Your True NORTH

A Guided Journal for Those Living with Cognitive Loss or Dementia about Legacy, Love and Wishes for the End of a Life Well-lived.

Anne Kenny, M.D.,
and Teresa Webb, R.N.

No part of this publication may be reproduced, stored in a retrieval system, or transmitted in any form or by any means—electronic, photocopying, recording, or otherwise—without prior written permission, except in the case of brief excerpts in critical reviews and articles. For permission requests, contact the author at DrAnne@TogetherinDementia.com.

All rights reserved.
Copyright © Anne Kenny

ISBN: 9798862578034

The author disclaims responsibility for adverse effects or consequences from the misapplication or injudicious use of the information contained in this book. Mention of resources and associations does not imply an endorsement.

To my family, immediate and extended.
With heartfelt gratitude for sharing all your gifts with me!

– Anne Kenny

My wife, DC, in the tapestry of life, you are the vibrant thread that has added color and depth to the fabric of my journey. Thank you for standing by me, cheering me on during the triumphs, and offering a comforting embrace during the trials. Your belief in me has been the catalyst for every success, and your love has been my refuge in times of doubt.

My beautiful daughter RM, your unwavering support and encouragement have been the fuel for my advocate endeavors. Through the highs and lows, your presence has been a constant source of inspiration, reminding me of the strength that lies within connections forged by heart and understanding.

My bestie, MD, In the novel of my life, you are the most cherished character, the sidekick who has stood by my side through every plot twist and narrative turn. Your friendship has been the ink that colors the pages of my story, and your encouragement has been the plot twist that turns challenges into triumphs.

DC, RM and MD, this dedication is a small token of gratitude for the countless ways you all have touched my life, leaving an indelible mark on the canvas of my existence.

– Teresa Webb

TABLE OF CONTENTS

Prologue 1
Writing from Teresa Webb 7
    The Elephant in the Room 7
    My Affairs 9
    Where is the Voice of the One Living with Dementia? 10
    The Other Me 11
    My Rights 12
    Gratitude to a True Friend 13
    Who Makes the Rules? 14
    Memory of the First Time 15
    Stigma 16
    Guidance 17

Chapter 1: Introduction 19
    The Kenny Family Story 19
    Living Well, Planning Well 21
    I See No Need to Discuss it, but It Helped My Son 23
        Bonnie and Ralph's Story 23
    Take Your Time and Think Broadly 25
    I Wish She Would Have Let Me Know 26
        Karen's story 26
        Let's Begin 27
    Points to Remember 29

Action Plan 30
Resources 31

Chapter 2: The Disease 33
The Kenny Family Story 33
Overview 34
Why Get A Diagnosis 37
What is Included in an Evaluation 39
    The History 40
    The Examination 45
    Testing That May Be Done 46
    What Can a Specialist Offer? 47
Brief Overview of Each Type of Dementia 48
What Recommendations Work to Keep Dementia at Bay? 51
Points to Remember 59
Action Plan 60
Resources 61

Chapter 3: Stigma 63
The Kenny Family Story 63
Kate Swaffer's Remarks on Stigma 66
Facing Our Fears and Our Prejudices 67
    Holly's Story 67
New Information on Stigma Informed
    by Those Living with Dementia 69
To Disclose or Not to Disclose the Diagnosis 71
What's to Risk if I Don't Disclose? 72
What Can be Done? Advocacy 73
    The Scotland Early Onset Alzheimer's
        Disease Group Story 74
The Quiet Advocate 74
The Consummate Teacher 75

    Dr. Walsh's Story 75
    Why We Need to Resist Stigma 77
    Points to Remember 79
    Action Plan 79
    Resources 80

Chapter 4: Communication and Communication Changes ... 81
    The Kenny Family Story 81
    Communication Changes Due to Dementia 82
    Strategies that May Help with Communication 83
    The Role of Speech Therapy in Cognitive Loss 85
    Expression Beyond Verbal Communication 85
        Tony and Doris' Story 86
    Augmentation to Verbal Communication 87
        Kelly and June 87
        Gina's story 89
    Expand your Communication Using the Arts 90
    Communication Around End-of-Life Wishes 92
        Sam and Lavonne's story 94
    Points to Remember 98
    Action Items 98
    Resources 99

Chapter 5: Legacy 101
    The Kenny Family Story 101
    Overview 102
    Legacy of Self 103
        Tony's Story 105
    Tangible Legacy or Keepsakes 107
        Kenny Family Story 107
        Photographs/Photo Albums or Audio Recordings ... 109
        Journals 110

    Jewelry/Furniture/Property/Land 110
    Books/Spiritual texts 110
    Hobbies (Sporting Goods/Tools/Hand Crafts) 111
Community Legacy 111
    Dr. W's Story 111
How to Leave this Legacy in a Time When Communication
    or Executive Function May be Impaired 115
Points to Remember 117
Action Plan 118
Resources 119

Chapter 6: Reflection 121
Overview 121
The Kenny Family Story 122
Why We Might Resist Reflection 122
Strategies to Get you Going 124
Reflections to Guide the Progression of the Disease 127
    Early Stages 127
    Reflections on Change 129
    Reflection on the Practical 130
Moderate Stages 130
    Preparing for Moderate Stages 131
    Senses 132
    Environment 136
Preparing for the End Stages 137
    Questions to Contemplate for the
        Late Stage of Dementia 139
    How to Reflect 141
    Medically 143
    Psychologically 144
    Spiritually 146
    Questions to Address When Considering
        Your Spirituality 148

Final Thoughts on Reflection..149
Points to Remember..150
Action Plan 151
Resources..151

Chapter 7: Values 153
The Kenny Family Story 153
Why Values? 155
Put Simply – How do YOU Want to Live? 156
Your Values as A Guide to Living Your Best Life................................157
Performing a Value Inventory 159
How Do You Accomplish a Life Review?..160
The Case for Following Your Values 166
The Five Core Values..167
How to Use the Values 167
    Mr. P and Sarah's Story 169
Future Planning..170
End-of-Life Choices 173
Points to Remember..178
Action Plan 179
Resources..179

Chapter 8: Planning and Preparing for Emotional and Physical Changes, Adaptations, and Limits 181
Overview 181
Palliative Approach to Quality of Life in Care 183
Emotions and Hope, Especially Around Initial Diagnosis 184
Planning..185
    Avoid Dehumanizing Treatment and Care 186
Usual Course of Late-Stage Dementia..189
    Eating/Swallowing.. 189

    Dehydration 190
    Infections 190
    Hospitalizations 191
    Terminal Agitation.. 192
Support in Confronting Emotionally
    Difficult Conversations 193
    Appraoch the Situation with a Curious
        and Respectful Mindset.. 193
    Concentrate on Listening, Rather than Speaking 194
    Be Direct 194
    Do Not Delay the Conversation.. 194
    Anticipate a Favorable Result... 194
Navigate Existential Tension 195
Defining Personal Autonomy 198
Addressing Lack of Confidence
    in the Healthcare System 199
    Openly Talking about Death, Planning,
        Exploring All Options 201
    What is Death and Dignity Legislation?................................ 204
Points to Remember..208
Action Plan 209
Resources..210

Chapter 9: Legal Considerations... 213
The Kenny Family Story 213
Overview 214
Estates and Finances...216
Planning for Healthcare..218
Keep Your Papers Accessible...219
Let Someone Know Where to Find
    Important Documents 222
Have the Discussions..222
Review and Update Your Plans Regularly...................................224

Other Considerations 224
   Organ Donation..224
   Funeral Plans..224
Advance Care Planning 225
A More Complete Living Will for Those
   Living with Dementia... 228
Communication with Others..230
Points to Remember...230
Action Plan 231
Resources...232

Chapter 10: Engaging with Family and the Healthcare System 233

The Kenny Family Story 233
Overview 235
The Problem with Building a Team..................................237
Facilitated Discussion with Family..................................240
Who is on Your Team? How Can You Enhance It?.......242
What are the Situations That May Need
   the Help of Friends/Family? 247
   Socialization/Adapting to Cognitive Loss................... 247
   Transportation 250
   Medication/Medical Coordination 253
   Administration/Finances 257
Connecting with Healthcare...258
Is Healthcare Even the Right Place to Address Care?............258
   Choosing a Healthcare Provider to Speak With........ 260
Understanding Hospice..264
   What if My Doctor Says it is Not Time?....................... 269
   Ideas for How to Have a Hospice Conversation
      with Your Team, Your Family, Your Health Care Proxy,
      and/or Your Physician 272

Points to Remember 273
Action Plan 274
Resources 275

PROLOGUE

Approximately 1.5 million new cases of dementia are estimated to be diagnosed in the US every year.[1] The number of individuals estimated to have Mild Cognitive Impairment due to Alzheimer's disease are 5-7 million US adults over age 65 years.[2] People with MCI due to Alzheimer's disease have biomarker evidence of Alzheimer's brain changes, along with new but subtle symptoms like memory issues, language difficulties, and trouble with thinking. These cognitive problems may be noticeable to the person themselves, their family, and friends, but not to others. And they might not get in the way of everyday activities.

While there is new hope on the horizon with research and new medications, dementia remains a progressive and fatal disease. It is the 6th leading cause of death and the 3rd leading cause of death in those over 80 years in the US.[3] The good news is that we can live long and well with the diagnosis of dementia. Initiatives such as Dementia Friendly America™[4] address this.

---

1 Alzheimer's Association. 2023 Alzheimer's Disease Facts and Figures. Alzheimers Dement 2023;19(4). DOI 10.1002/alz.13016. p 25-28.
2 Alzheimer's Association. 2023 Alzheimer's Disease Facts and Figures. Alzheimers Dement 2023;19(4). DOI 10.1002/alz.13016 pg.23
3 Alzheimer's Association. 2023 Alzheimer's Disease Facts and Figures. Alzheimers Dement 2023;19(4).
4 https://www.dfamerica.org/

Unfortunately, dying well with dementia has not received as much attention. It is the norm to avoid discussions of death. Therefore, making decisions about end-of-life wishes are left to those partnering in care for those individuals who have lost their voice to dementia. But the tide is shifting. Atul Gawande's *Being Mortal* and my book, *Making Tough Decisions about End-of-Life Care in Dementia* suggest that we can choose alternatives to persistent medical care and shift our focus to value-based, goal-directed care.

To do this, we must have conversations for the goals for our deaths. Resources such as The Conversation Project[5] and Death over Dinner[6] provide a framework for these conversations but families may not engage.

The purpose of this book is to move the needle on discussion about wishes for end-of-life care for those newly diagnosed with MCI or dementia. My first attempt at moving the needle approached the subject with the fact and the figures, but I shocked and traumatized my audiences. I learned a direct approach was too blunt. Next, I peppered humor into my delivery, much as Sheila Nevins, American television producer and previous President of HBO Documentary Films, did when discussing making a last will and testament in an PBS Newshour commentary[7], but those discussions also fell flat.

I took time to contemplate how the discussion could move forward. As a geriatric and palliative care physician, I realized what I had done over 30 years in practice to become comfortable

---

[5] https://theconversationproject.org/
[6] https://deathoverdinner.org/
[7] Sheila Nevins' PBS Newshour commentary about creating last will and testament. https://www.pbs.org/newshour/show/why-writing-my-last-will-and-testament-called-for-an-ice-cream-sundae

discussing deeper, vulnerable conversations was to take time, begin with values and allow time for reflection. Finally, finding the best way to communicate, sometimes in brief talks at opportune moments or through writing with a request for a follow-up discussion when the recipient had the gift of time for reflection. More paced, tempered, reflective interactions through writing and speech to navigate goals and wishes. No shock, no trauma. Just values and wishes shared and communicated for a treasured ending to a life well lived.

And the second thing I realized was helpful, for me and for my patients, was telling the stories of other people with dementia and how they handled their decisions and their lives. I know that it is important to hear about an experience from someone who has lived it. So, the second goal of this book is to hear from those who have lived life with cognitive loss.

I am fortunate that Teresa Webb has collaborated with me on this book. Here are the words of Teresa:

My career as a dedicated registered nurse was marked by unwavering dedication to my patients' well-being. Compassionate care and empathetic approach earned me the love and trust of countless individuals and families. However, my life took an unexpected turn when I received a diagnosis of Primary Progressive Aphasia, a variant of FrontoTemporal Dementia (FTD). Rather than allowing this diagnosis to define me, I learned to embrace this new reality with courage and resilience; in doing so, I became an advocate for dementia awareness and compassionate end-of-life care.

Amidst the challenges that dementia brings, I recognized the pressing need for open communication about end-of-life wants and needs. With a deeper understanding of the complexities that arise as dementia progresses, I have embarked on a mission to empower individuals and their families to have meaningful conversations about their wishes.

Founding the FrontoTemporal Dementia Advocacy Resource Network (FTDARN) was a pivotal moment in my advocacy journey. Through this nonprofit, a lifeline of support and education for those affected by FTD has been created. My vision was to foster a community where individuals and their families could find solace, information, and a sense of belonging amidst the challenges posed by FTD.

My dedication extends beyond national borders. As a public and international speaker, I have traversed the globe, sharing my story, insights, and the importance of open communication. My words have resonated with audiences of diverse backgrounds, igniting conversations that are beginning to transform the way we approach dementia care and end-of-life planning.

Below, I candidly share my personal experiences, fears, and triumphs, inviting readers to join me on a voyage of understanding and empathy. It is my hope these stories, intertwine with the voices of fellow advocates and experts, reveal the transformative impact of honest conversations about end-of-life care. I believe my journey demonstrates that open communication is a gift that not only empowers individuals with dementia but also enriches the lives of their loved ones.

As we delve deeper into the narratives of those touched by dementia, we celebrate the unwavering commitment to advocacy, a pioneering spirit in fostering dialogue, and an unshakeable belief in the power of empathy. Through the pages of this book, I am reminded that by embracing vulnerability and

PROLOGUE

engaging in compassionate conversations, we pave the way for a more inclusive, understanding, and supportive society.

Join us on this enlightening expedition as we embark on a collective journey to change perceptions, transform lives, and create a world where the voices of those with dementia are heard, cherished, and valued.

You will hear her voice at the beginning of the book and my voice in the chapters that follow.

In addition to Teresa's voice, the voices of individuals living with dementia who have authored memoirs are included. Each chapter will include writing excerpts from several authors who live with dementia. Their voices inform the material that is provided.

Though Teresa and I have different voices, we share a common vision and mission. We, Teresa and I, pray that you find this information helpful and provides practical information to guide your decisions and reflections, to assist in communicating your wishes and in living your best life.

WRITING FROM TERESA WEBB

The Elephant in the Room

For many of us diagnosed with dementia of any variant, what is feared most is the burden that we feel will be placed on family and our closest friends during the later stages of our disease. Some of us even go to the extreme of planning our own death, not because of a mental diagnosis (depression, etc.), but because we want to be able to control what happens and when it happens in order to lessen the burden, we feel we have become. It's the elephant in the middle of the room, not to be discussed with family or even "normal" friends, those who are not living with a diagnosis. It's our new friends, the ones who can so relate to these dark feelings, those who are living with dementia, who we turn to for understanding. It's a safe place where we become each other's confidant. You can find us in our secret groups on social media, where we openly and honestly discuss what we cannot with family and others: how to die with dignity and on our terms. One member of a secret group, Kim, was upset because she tried to speak with her daughter about not posting pictures of her in later stages or as she neared death. Kim had been reading on other dementia sites where caregivers showed pictures of their loved ones bedridden, emaciated, some with a blank stare, others sitting alone in adult-sized feeding chairs with captions saying anything from "Look what my spouse, family member etc. has become" to "How long do you think he/she will live looking like this." Kim's daughter said she was not ready to talk about death, and Kim waited almost a year before her daughter was ready to begin having numerous conversations about what Kim wanted and did not want as her disease progressed.

In another secret group we would meet via video chat every week to check in with each other. This group was formed because someone who was diagnosed with early onset of Alzheimer's took their own life. This person was young, in their 40s, and had a loving spouse and young children. Yes, it's terrible and "poor thing." But here is what those in the group understood: This precious person felt as though there was no other way to control her life. Death would be releasing the family from financial ruin and becoming a huge burden. No longer would this person wake each morning wondering which of her abilities would be lost. As time went on, those of us left behind began to wonder if this person initiated their death too soon. Maybe a conversation about what was important to them would have put everyone at ease, to just breathe and move on to find a new place in life/society. I mean, just because we are diagnosed doesn't mean we are dead already. We know what the outcome is. We are aware of what the present has brought us to and what it has left behind. We still have feelings, and in the newness of our disease, it can feel like we are tomcats trying to get out of a burlap bag. The world as we knew it has ceased to exist. There are so many questions, and fear of the answers.

My Affairs

When I look back during the early time of my diagnosis, I did not weep, I did not ask "Why me?" To me there was no time to look at and digest what my kind and compassionate neurologist handed me: a forever life-changing diagnosis. Primary progressive aphasia (PPA), a variant of frontotemporal dementia (FTD), prognosis 2-6 years. My daughter Renee on my left and my wife Denise on my right both sat silent. He looked at all three of us and said to me "I cannot tell you what is going on inside your house (my brain), I can only tell you what the outside looks like, and you need to get your affairs in order as soon as you can." Renee thanked him and took my hand. I can remember looking at Denise and seeing something in her eyes. Fear? Sadness? It was a look that told me my "affairs" would need to address some hard truths about our end-of-life decisions.

"Our end-of-life decisions." No one wants to talk about end-life choices and how to honor what is requested. I see it as not just my choices, but it involves those whom I choose to follow my wishes and requests, that being my daughter and my wife. What if you can no longer chew? What if you need 24-hour care? What if you can no longer communicate your needs – how will I know what to do? So many questions, so many options are out there to think about. These are questions that we had to ask ourselves and to discuss with a lot of love and patience. It was apparent that we all were beginning to accept not only the disease but what the end stages of this disease will bring because, we were actually discussing and not just "agreeing for the sake of ending an uncomfortable topic."

Where is the Voice of the One Living with Dementia?

A famous celebrity has just been diagnosed with FTD, and it is a media blitz; every television station, radio, social media is covering some sort of story. The celebrity had made an announcement 10 months before about retiring due to a diagnosis of aphasia. I asked in my small support group at the time what they all thought of the diagnosis. We sat and discussed whether this person could have had a stroke that left them with some sort of aphasia? Did this person sustain some sort of traumatic brain injury? We all agreed that for whatever reason, the celebrity was going to have a different journey in life. Then a few weeks ago, the same celebrity's family stated the celebrity had progressed and now has FTD. The family stated this, but where was the celebrity and his voice? Where was the lived experience? The voice and opinion of the person living with the disease, actually dealing with the disease every day, is often left out of the media and medical community and policymaker's comments and opinions. The next day, a high-level executive along with a member of the medical advisory board went on national news to discuss FTD. Again, where was the lived experience? Why wasn't someone from the lived experience advisory committee invited to share? That same day, I had received a voice mail from the same organization asking if I would discuss my lived experience with the local media. Before I could return the call, I received an email as a follow up again asking if I would share my FTD story. The marketing and communications team was encouraging local media outlets to feature people willing to speak about their own personal experiences along with local physicians who were knowledgeable about FTD. ... The next paragraph asked whether I would be comfortable contacting "your loved ones' doctor to join you." Weeks went by, yet no one contacted me. How cruel can one get? Is it any wonder that the dementia stigma isn't going away? The only time the lived experience means anything is if you can't remember your age or have such extreme movements that even a walker is dangerous to use. Then it seems it's OK to speak about the lived experience. But wait, you need to have a family member and your physician sit next to you so they can speak for you. Is it any wonder we must continually push to have a voice? So often we are treated as though we are the monkeys brought out only when the organ grinder comes out to play. The cruelty of this disease is not only the disease itself but those who use us to exploit their hidden agendas, line their pockets, or both.

The Other Me

During dinner clean-up the other day, I shared with Denise that I have noticed I am having increased short term memory issues. We talked a little about memory challenges, and then she said, "You know I cannot remember you before your diagnosis." I really was not expecting that. Even though we have been married for 17 years, we have been on the dementia journey for 13 years. My heart fell a little, and I felt such guilt. Each minute, hour, day, that has gone by has not only robbed me of myself, but it has robbed Denise of the person she fell in love with. Sometimes I look in the mirror and ask, "Who am I today?" It is true that as time goes on, we change – our ideas, looks, etc. – but it's that I cannot truly remember the other me, the one that had a "normal" brain, or did I really ever have a normal brain?

My Rights

I received a telephone call from the local election's office. There was a voice mail stating they had questions related to my signature on a ballot and would I "give us a call back." The gentleman's voice sounded as though he was unsure of what he was saying because there was such hesitation in his voice. But, just hearing they were questioning my signature was enough to bring my darkest fear to the surface. However, I did return the elections office call. Because of this fear, my words were slightly slurred and there was a lot of hesitation when speaking. I asked why this office was now calling me about my signature. They said, "Your signature is different from how you signed your voter registration card." I told the gentleman that I had a disability which changes my signature depending on how my day is. This insensitive man had the nerve to ask what my disability was. My heart began to pound so hard I thought it would jump out from my chest. My Lord, this is an "at will," and I did not want to share my diagnosis for fear that someone would report me, and I would lose another freedom, to drive. I know many people feel that as soon as you have a diagnosis you are to give up everything, driving being one of those. However, I feel it is only a matter of time before the right to vote will be snatched away. Yes, my signature is different than it used to be and yes, I keyboard rather than cursive so that I can communicate. I feel it was very intrusive to have someone question and ask what my disability is. Dementia is more than a diagnosis. It is a way of life; it is the end of many freedoms that "normal" people do not consider. When I told my daughter about the election office, she asked me why I was so upset. I told her that I feared it was just a matter of time before people with dementia would not be allowed to vote. There was a pause on the phone and then she said, "Oh Mom, I never even would consider that. I am so sorry."

Gratitude to a True Friend

Dear John [my friend and dance partner],

It is with a heart full of gratitude and love that I thank you for being such an understanding and compassionate human. While I was rehabbing from a craniotomy for a brain aneurysm, you would telephone often, always telling me not to despair as I was going to dance again. Right! Does he not understand I was learning to walk, feed, and dress myself, and what was up with my speech? But you kept the calls short because I was unable to speak clearly. But taking your time, slowing your words, we spoke about dance, as you knew it was my passion. My physical therapist kept saying I would never dance again, I would always need a walking device, telling me that "it was up to me." It was shortly after I received my PPA diagnosis that you convinced me to come to the dance studio, "Just to visit" you said. I remember walking into the studio and feeling something I was not sure of, but it felt good. My wife handed me a bag containing practice clothes and shoes, saying "Time to get ready." Get ready? I thought, I am using a cane and have no balance. But "it was up to me." John, when you held out your hand and said, "Leave the cane and come with me," when my shoes touched the wood floor, I remember experiencing such excitement, the excitement of feeling hope. I got into the frame, taking a deep breath in as I performed a 3 of a Natural [A natural turn is a dance step in which the partners turn around each other clockwise; the 3 denotes standard to explain the beat, the foot position, alignment, the amount of turn and footwork], the initial standard waltz step, then moving along the floor. You would stop and ask me "What'd you do?" Even though I could not remember the name of the dance figure, I looked directly in your eyes and replied, "I moved my feet." With a smile and hug, you told me as long as I can move my feet, I can dance. When I shared my PPA diagnosis with you, your loving wife gave me the first of many journal articles on muscle memory. She would encourage me to learn as much as I could. Never mind the figure names, close your eyes and just move. John, I remember those long hours you spent preparing me for what would be my last dance competition. Walking without a cane, we danced all 10 dances at a gold level, as my physical therapist sat in the audience to witness what hope, compassion, determination, and empowerment could do. While it's been 10 years since we have danced, the memory of how you treated me with such kindness, compassion and respect still remains.

Who Makes the Rules?

What does "Death with Dignity" mean to me? This is a question that I have asked myself numerous times. Looking back at my nursing years, I cannot say what I used to think because there is a blank space where those memories were. I can only answer from where I am today, or each day that I think about that question. I think death with dignity is a personal choice. I don't think there are rules, but rather I do think that there is moral tendency to believe there is. I remember when I was in college, I attended a private nursing college that promoted "excellence in patient care." This included dying with dignity. I had often wondered who made up the rules for this? Wasn't it really a personal choice of what dying meant to a person? I asked my daughter who she thinks makes up the rules for dying with dignity, or are there any rules? She stated that it's ethics boards and, in some states, it is the state. I asked her how could the ethics board know what I think it is, or does it not count? She was quiet and then said, "But Mom, I already know what you want." I told her that if I was to follow the rules some board had made to govern and say what dying with dignity is, how could she follow my wishes? She said that she thought the state and ethics board made sure that someone with depression or mental illness did not commit suicide. We discussed how this plays into PLWD. In most states where "assisted death" is legal, it is legal for everyone **except** those that have been diagnosed with dementia. It seems as though when a person has dementia stamped on their forehead, they lose so many "rights," even the right to orchestrate the timing of their own demise.

Memory of the First Time

The first human I ever saw dead was my dad. I was 14 years old, and he was lying in a casket in a room with heavy drapes and a few lamps with pink lightbulbs. For whatever reason, the old film of him laying for public display so that those who came to say goodbye would have "one last memory" of him never really goes away. I remember sitting on a chair looking at the line of people patiently waiting their turn to say a final goodbye. Whenever I go back to those memories, I am still filled with the same questions. Did my dad have a dignifying death? Why was he dressed in a suit and put on display for everyone to say goodbye? My dad never wore a suit – he wore jean overalls most days or some kind of men's work pants. But a navy blue suit and white shirt was not what he would have wanted to wear, never mind being on public display.

As I pondered why the mourners came to see my dad when he was dead but were not there when he was alive baffled me. To me this is one reason why when someone is diagnosed with dementia, the discussion about what is meaningful, how they want to die with dignity, what does end of life mean to them should occur. They can let people know if they want visitors and jeans rather than a blue suit. All the dark and scary stuff needs to come front and center, because once a light is shed on the dark and scary, it is no longer so. Then PLWD can begin to really live in the moment without worrying if they will become a corpse laying in a box with the lid open for public display. Why do people come for the final goodbye? Should they not come while the person is still living? Wouldn't that last visit be one of meaning and make a lasting memory?

Why is it assumed the PLWD cannot speak for themselves in regards to their end-of-life wishes or even how/what they want for health care on their life journey? Early onset or not, it feels as though once you are diagnosed, you magically become invisible, unseen, no voice.

Stigma

I have been privileged to be a part of a Community Review for pilot research grant applications. These grant applications are to find innovative ways to advance care in the emergency department for PLWD and their care partners. How is it that I can read, score, and summarize each grant, attend meetings where my voice is heard and respected, but yet when it comes to my personal wishes in regards to my healthcare, my voice is silenced by those who can talk over and above me, as if I am not there? As I am reading a few grant reviews, it surprises me that some researchers have the nerve to state that PLWD may be unable to answer "SIMPLE" questions. This kind of language is not OK. It is humiliating and demeaning at best to think no matter what the education, PLWD continue to be stigmatized.

Guidance

When I was first diagnosed (2010), my wife Denise and I were encouraged to find and go to a support group. There were not support groups held in the neurologist's office, and later we were told no one in the office knew of any. I felt so helpless that I could not help the one person who was about to embark on a journey that she had no clue where my dementia would take her. One evening she said she found a support group and was going to attend. A short time later she returned and said it wasn't the "right kind" of support group. All the caregivers were much older than she and their loved ones all had aphasia that stemmed from a stroke! I felt guilty, I felt sad for my wife. She needed someone to talk to, she needed to know what to do, and she needed to know she was not alone. Realizing at that time there was no support, no resources for myself or my wife, we eventually muddled through trying to navigate all the streets that had no names. While there are many support types of groups now, a piece that is still missing is a resource book for the newly diagnosed, their family and community, to include their healthcare providers. I wish there was a *Your True North* book when I was diagnosed. It would have been much easier to navigate life.

Chapter 1

INTRODUCTION

The Kenny Family Story

Interesting things are at the edge or border – we are at the edge with regard to how to approach end-of-life care for ourselves. With the advances in medicine, we live longer, but do we always live better? My grandmother, a woman born in the century that witnessed the Civil War, knew that life was finite. She lived it every day in her work as a nurse, housewife, mother, and neighbor in the rural Midwest. To feed her family, she understood animals were slaughtered and gardens grew and then went fallow. She was a nurse in World War I, the 1917 influenza pandemic, and she witnessed infant mortality and death during childbirth. She watched people, young and old, deserving and undeserving, die. My grandmother came to live with us for a time when I was a pre-adolescent. She didn't stay more than two years – she missed the country and the country lifestyle. As I sat in her room learning to sew and mend, she answered questions about her life and rendered her opinions when I commented, "That is sad." She would say, "No, it is just what is dealt. What is sad is when we cannot abide by what comes into our path."

Now, we shop in grocery stores and families are often more spread out. As Ezekial Emanuael, MD, PhD, an oncologist, bio-ethicist, and Professor of Medicine, points out, we have a notion that we are immortal. It is no longer just young people who see life as going on and on ... all of us do.[8] But now we are at an edge – one that we have given over to the medical profession but that we need to take back and think about. Mary Pipher, American clinical psychologist and author of 'Women Rowing North and Writing to Change the World' says, "Borders teem with life, color, and complexity. In nature, we find the most diversity where ecosystems merge.[9]" Death isn't just about health and medicine, but the merging of spirit, mind, and body – we need to take back the complexity of choosing how to live and choosing how to die.

This book is intended for those who have been given the diagnosis of dementia: Alzheimer's, vascular, Lewy body, FrontoTemporal, early onset, or late onset or the diagnosis of mild cognitive impairment (MCI). Some saw it coming and others did not. Those around them may have seen it coming and others may not have. We all cope in different ways, and the disease affects all in different ways.

There are commonalities to what people are told when they are diagnosed with dementia. In the audience at recent meetings of the Dementia Action Alliance and the Dementia Alliance

---

8 https://www.theatlantic.com/magazine/archive/2014/10/why-i-hope-to-die-at-75/379329/
9 Pg 111 Writing to Change the World

INTRODUCTION

International, I heard many living with dementia report that along with the diagnosis, they were told, "There is nothing we can do. Take a pill and come back to see the us (medical community) in six months to a year". Others were told, "Put your affairs in order," and were left to wonder what that really means.

So many people with dementia experience psychological distress in the period after diagnosis.[10] For those who were given support (and hope), this reported distress markedly decreased from 30% that reported distress to only 5% reporting distress while those left without support, the psychological distress increased from a baseline of 30% reporting distress to 45% that reported distress in the next 6 months.[11]

Living Well, Planning Well

But many individuals living with dementia have given us guidance that there is so much to live for – legacy, advocacy, community. There are changes, to be sure, but there are hundreds and hundreds of success stories – and hopefully, one day soon, thousands and thousands. There is little written by those living with dementia, but when present ...they are gems. Richard Taylor, Ph.D., author of *Alzheimer's from the Inside Out*, was one of the first individuals living with dementia to write, blog, and advocate for the voices of those living with dementia. He reminds us, "From the mind and heart of someone who has

---

10 Petty, S., Harvey, K., Griffiths, A., Coleston, D. M., & Dening, T. (2018). Emotional distress with dementia: A systematic review using corpus-based analysis and meta-ethnography. *International journal of geriatric psychiatry*, 33(5), 679-687.

11 Justyna Mazurek, Dorota Szcześniak, Katarzyna Małgorzata Lion, Rose-Marie Dröes, Maciej Karczewski & Joanna Rymaszewska (2019) Does the Meeting Centres Support Programme reduce unmet care needs of community-dwelling older people with dementia? A controlled, 6-month follow-up Polish study, Clinical Interventions in Aging, 14:, 113-122, DOI: 10.2147/CIA.S185683

Alzheimer's disease, there are lots of questions and very few answers."

This book is about living well with dementia, and specifically about planning for the transition you would like to see when you've articulated what is no longer living well and you begin to die from this disease (or another). So how do we navigate this journey? I have found wisdom in a small book by Richard Bode, *First You Have to Row a Little Boat*. In the introduction after describing the loss of his parents when he was still a boy, Mr. Bode states, "All that happened to me a half century ago, and I survived. In the intervening years I have discovered that – despite the overwhelming nature of that early disaster – day-to-day life isn't a constant series of crises and calamities. Day-to-day life is like the wind in all its infinite variations and moods. The wind is shifting, constantly shifting, blowing north northeast, then northeast, then north – just as we, ourselves, are constantly shifting, sometimes happy, sometimes angry, sometimes sad. As the sailor sails his winds, so we must sail our moods." And I would say, the course of this disease is as unpredictable as the wind. We don't always get to pick the vagrancies of life, and after we've adjusted to the new diagnosis, how do we spend the day-to-day? This may be the secret to a life well-lived with dementia – the day-to-day, adapting, adjusting, and reevaluating.

Planning can help with some of the journey with dementia. Many do plan for many aspects of dying such as mapping out a funeral, the songs, letters to loved ones, and legal aspects of money and possessions. When these details are attended to, most report improved feelings about accomplishing these tasks.[12] Planning for the other aspects of the time in late dementia, prior to death, is reportedly more difficult for several reasons that we will review in the chapters to come.[13] Making decisions for oneself may not help you, but families report less stress, depression, and anxiety when wishes of their family member have been communicated.[14]

I See No Need to Discuss It, But It Helped My Son

Bonnie and Ralph's Story

Ralph walked in the door, a bit stooped and sheepish. He stated he had someone with his mother, Bonnie, so that he could prepare me for what he hoped would happen during my upcoming scheduled time to speak with Bonnie. Ralph had been to lectures and had read my book, Making Tough Decisions about End-of-Life Care in Dementia. But Ralph didn't know how to bring up the discussion of Bonnie's wishes with her, and he was worried she would progress before he could gather the courage to ask. Ralph had told his mother that her primary care physician, Dr Smith, wanted Bonnie to see me. Ralph further asked if I could broach the topic with Bonnie without him in the room as he was worried about her emotional response and that Ralph would have difficulty hearing what Bonnie had to say. After

---

12 Dickinson, C., Bamford, C., Exley, C., Emmett, C., Hughes, J., & Robinson, L. (2013). Planning for tomorrow whilst living for today: the views of people with dementia and their families on advance care planning. International Psychogeriatrics, 25(12), 2011-2021.

13 Sellars, M., Chung, O., Nolte, L., Tong, A., Pond, D., Fetherstonhaugh, D., ... & Detering, K. M. (2019). Perspectives of people with dementia and carers on advance care planning and end-of-life care: A systematic review and thematic synthesis of qualitative studies. Palliative medicine, 33(3), 274-290.

14 Detering, K. M., Hancock, A. D., Reade, M. C., & Silvester, W. (2010). The impact of advance care planning on end of life care in elderly patients: randomised controlled trial. Bmj, 340

telling me of his private concerns, Ralph and I found Bonnie waiting to have lunch in the day program. She reluctantly rose and walked with me to my office; Ralph remained chatting with the others in the day program. Bonnie, bright-eyed but dubious, began reluctantly with introductions. She asked, "Why do Ralph and Dr. Smith want me to speak with you? Am I dying?" After I assured her that she was not, we began a discussion of her life, her passions, her loves. "Bonnie, what is your greatest accomplishment?" Bonnie beamed, "My children. Raising my children." "Any regrets or relationships you feel need attention?" I asked. Bonnie took a long pause. Slowly and deliberately, she answered, "No – I think people like me, respect me, and I think I've shown respect to others." Further discussion revealed she did not have any unfinished business or wishes. I turned to wishes for medical care as her disease progressed. Bonnie bristled. "I don't see why I have to talk about this. I don't really like that you're asking." I assured Bonnie we did not have to talk about it. We called Ralph into the room to recap and say our goodbyes. Ralph, still looking sheepish, heard that his mother was proud of her life, and he was visibly moved that her greatest accomplishment was raising her children. Hearing that revelation gave Ralph the strength to ask tough questions. He touched his mother's arm and inquired, "Could you talk about a few questions I have if you were to get sick? I'm afraid I don't know what you'd want me to do, and I don't want to do it wrong." Bonnie nodded. Ralph asked, "What if you get a really bad pneumonia – would you want to go to the hospital and have that treated?" Bonnie shook her head slowly, "No, I don't want things like that treated." "A heart attack?" Ralph pressed. Bonnie looked up and looked Ralph directly in the eye. "No son,

INTRODUCTION

I want to stay put and comfortable, with you." Ralph smiled. "It really helps me to hear that."

Take Your Time and Think Broadly

It doesn't happen overnight – knowing your plan. We avoid discussion of the messy parts of life. There is a reluctance to have discussions about death – both those dealing with death and those who support them don't "want to lose hope or feel as if we are giving up."[15] John Abraham, in *How to Get the Death You Want*, states "People tend to build up fears about topics hidden from them, and these fears grow to be worse than the realities. Death is a biological reality, a cultural phenomenon, a spiritual event, an economic reality, and a psychological process. The topic is taboo in our society, making it important to address the reality of death seriously, realistically, and helpfully." Thus, death is a complex time of life. And death is not a part of life that conforms to plans. But consider some broad brush strokes. People living with dementia report that they do not want to be "locked into a pathway" by discussing or documenting their end-of-life wishes, that it is "just ticking certain boxes on a pathway predefined by health professionals."[16] But, this is not the type of process I want you to consider. This process and these conversations need to be thoughts or discussions, tempered by reflection and then revisited and refined. They are broad – encompassing legacy, communication, community, spirit, faith, hope, and love – not whether or not there will be artificial breathing

---

[15] Fetherstonhaugh D, McAuliffe L, Bauer M, Shanley C. Decision-making on behalf of people living with dementia: how do surrogate decision-makers decide? J Med Ethics. 2017 Jan;43(1):35-40. doi: 10.1136/medethics-2015-103301. Epub 2016 Oct 25. PMID: 27780889

[16] Sellars et al Palliative Medicine 2019

or nutrition. The "answers" for the doctors of whether and when there is artificial anything comes after the reflection and refinement. This is not a race; neither can it be put off. This disease, because of its characteristics and effects on the brain, must be dealt with long before most of us are ready to have the discussion.

The discussion may not happen – but then we are left with others making the decisions – whether it is the healthcare community or family. Many people I speak to report that they do not want to be a burden. I contend that the best way to avoid being a burden is to articulate specific wishes. Most families would happily and devotedly care for their families but have tremendous trouble making life and death decisions for them. This is a great gift – to clearly articulate what is wanted and when.

I Wish She Would Have Let Me Know

Karen's story

Karen is a quiet, slight woman with dark black hair. She sits across from me in a quiet room. "Thank you for seeing me. I know you haven't seen me for over a year, but I've been so unsettled since my mother died. She always told me I would know what to do, but I'm haunted by whether I caused her death." Alma had been a deeply spiritual woman, a pillar in her faith community. She was surrounded by community as she lived with dementia and had great faith that God would care for her until her death and after. Karen had been her surrogate decision-maker and had asked Alma what she had wanted as her Alzheimer's disease progressed. All Alma would say was, "You'll know what to do." Karen asked me for a meeting at the *prompting of her mother's faith community due to her distress over such a prolonged period of time.* "I have so many questions. At the time, how to help my mother seemed so unclear and I thought she would not want to linger with her condition. She seemed so tired, and eating was a struggle. But now I wonder if I should have done more for her, and would that have kept her alive longer?"

Karen's story highlights the difficulty of being a surrogate decision-maker. The burden for Karen was not assisting in the care of her mother, but in the decisions at the end of her life. Making decisions for other people's life and death increases the risk for depression, anxiety, and post-traumatic stress disorder.[17] And having the support of palliative care and others doesn't seem to help in alleviating the distress. Having a frank discussion with family or leaving some type of message (whether via notes, letters, or video recordings) can be a great relief.

Let's Begin

Malcolm Gladwell, an English-born Canadian journalist, author and public speaker, says a story needs to transport you – take you somewhere you haven't been before.[18] I am hoping this text does that – to some familiar places, but to places that we are often afraid to go. I find that if someone goes with me, I am not as afraid to tread to a new area. I am at a transition time in my life – often alone, as begins to happen more and more as we age. I sometimes venture off on my own, but not uncommonly

---

[17] Carson, S. S., Cox, C. E., Wallenstein, S., Hanson, L. C., Danis, M., Tulsky, J. A., ... & Nelson, J. E. (2016). Effect of palliative care–led meetings for families of patients with chronic critical illness: a randomized clinical trial. *Jama, 316*(1), 51-62.

[18] https://www.masterclass.com/articles/malcolm-gladwells-tips-for-structuring-a-story-like-the-ketchup-conundrum

ask one of my adult children or a friend to come with me – just to make it less frightening. I recently rented a tiller to prepare a patch of yard for a parking pad. For the first time, I would be hooking up a trailer hitch, driving in the car with the trailer behind, and using the ramps that I had made with a ramp kit. My son, who had agreed to help with the tilling, shoveling, and supervising of the teenage help, chuckled when I asked him to come early to escort me to pick up the tiller. He knows me. He knows just by standing by he is doing me a huge service. He maintains a light mood, smiles each time I look over at him tentatively, lets me try, listens to me whimper and whine, will offer to do it, and then stand back as I gain the courage to do all these new steps myself. That is what I hope I can do as I prod you to review your goals and dreams and prepare to share with family or friends that may be needed to assist in your life going forward. And my prayer for you is that you'll have someone as gracious as my son (any of my kids really – this one just happens to star in this story) to stand by; ready to step in if needed, but not too soon.

Richard Taylor, Ph.D., in *Alzheimer's from the Inside Out*, makes an analogy of Alzheimer's disease progression to a play with three acts and an intermission. In Act One, only you and a few very close to you know that you have Alzheimer's disease. You then enter an intermission "for an indeterminate period of time" and, as Dr. Taylor describes, "You have a vague idea what is going to happen in the next act, but you don't talk about it because it might ruin it for other people who didn't understand the first act. You know that awareness of the play ends with Act Two, but you will still be the star of Act Three. In fact, many of those sitting around you know the same fact, but it just doesn't seem appropriate to talk about that right now." And so, the process of talking about it and preparing for the changes likely falls to you. Dr. Taylor goes on to say, "There are checklists, books, tapes, seminars, study groups, web sites, and on and on and on and on. Each and all of these offer answers. Most of these answers are directed to the questions of caregivers. Very few of the answers claim to answer the questions of individuals living with the diagnosis. ... Most people offer answers to their own questions, not mine. My questions, when answered by others, sound and feel to me as if people are avoiding my concerns and concentrating on their own 'issues'."

So, let's begin. Let's see if we can find some questions and answers that make sense for you and find a way to communicate the answers or the follow-up questions to family, carers, healthcare providers, advocates, policymakers, friends, or whoever you need to speak to. Let's tell some stories.

Points to Remember

- Dementia is a chronic, progressive, degenerative disease. There are many years that may be lived well – there is much to be hopeful for, even in the face of this new diagnosis.
- Having psychological support in the period following the diagnosis of dementia markedly helps in adapting to the diagnosis.
- Planning assists in creating and maintaining your life and your goals, including preparing for your wishes in the late stage of dementia.
- This is not a race; neither can it be put off. This disease, because of its characteristics and effects on the brain, must

be dealt with far long before most of us are ready to have the discussion. Making your decisions and wishes known will help those who need to implement the wishes deal with the responsibility.

Action Plan

- Begin noticing how best you communicate. Writing, speaking, art, music? Does using a movie's message help you bridge the awkwardness of a difficult conversation? Just begin to notice so that you can use this information as you explore your wishes and seek a way to communicate them to others.

- Make a list of people who can be used as resources as you ponder planning for a time in the distant future. Suggestions include a friend, clergy, physician, psychotherapist, and/or person from a different generation (for some new ideas/perspective). Who might you just bounce ideas off of, who can listen while you muse, who has no skin in the game, no emotional or other attachments and can just hear you ponder?

- Begin to explore your opinions about care with advanced dementia. Journal on your thoughts and questions. What are your core beliefs about life? What are your core beliefs about death? Your experience with others around illness, dementia, or death? Do you think of death as always bad? Can you imagine when death may be preferable to life? As you contemplate your questions, review the physiological changes that accompany dementia, and the spiritual aspects of facing death.

INTRODUCTION

Resources

Richard Taylor, *Alzheimer's from the Inside Out*

This is a first-person narrative of short pieces and essays written by a man living with early-onset dementia. Dr. Taylor is a co-founder of Dementia Action Alliance, a non-profit national advocacy and education organization of people living with dementia, care partners, friends, and dementia specialists committed to creating a better country in which to live with dementia.

Richard Bore, *First You Have to Row a Little Boat: Reflections on Life and Living*

"Written by a grown man looking back on his childhood, it reflects on what learning to sail taught him about life: making choices, adapting to change, and becoming his own person." The last is a description by the publishers. It is a beautiful, small book written by someone who has been through enough difficulties to ring true when life sends difficulties, such as a new diagnosis of dementia.

Chapter 2

THE DISEASE

The Kenny Family Story

My sister accompanied my mom to her appointment with the geriatric specialist. The signs that something was wrong had been evident for a few years – suspicions by most of my siblings were high. My mom was visiting the bank several times a week, if not daily, due to anxiety around bills and balances. There were more and more fast food meals rather than planning, shopping, and cooking. The wide circle of friends and numerous outings were shrinking to a few friends willing to drive Mom and withstand the repeated calls confirming the appointment she had written on her calendar. I had done some preliminary cognitive testing the year before, but the screen had not shown evidence of cognitive impairment. More in-depth neuropsychological testing and negative laboratory results suggested dementia, a likely mix of Alzheimer's disease and a vascular component. The news was shocking to my mother, but she had several factors in her favor. Her physician was knowledgeable and compassionate, and my sister was positive, supportive, and resourceful. My mother was given the message of hope and adjustments. My sister asked my mother what her goals were, what gave her meaning and happiness – my mother reported independence and time with friends and family engaged in interesting activities. My sister worked with my mother to provide safe medication delivery, simplified my mother's meal planning and wardrobe, and helped her schedule time and activities with friends and family. And these adaptations worked for quite a while. In time, my mother's driving was tested by an independent driving evaluator and found to be lacking. A shift to an assisted living environment, where she would be driven to activities and where a few of her friends lived, was arranged. My mother was enjoying her life. And sprinkled into the independence, activities, visits, and moves, we had discussions about what she would want done as the disease worsened. My mother had been alive when cancer diagnoses were kept from people. She always said she would want to know if she had cancer or another terminal disease, that she believed in hospice and knowing when "enough was enough." She repeatedly made it clear that when she moved to the last stage of dementia, she would want loving support, not life-sustaining treatments.

Overview

"What is dementia?" Dementia refers to a group of diseases that affect the brain and cause cognitive difficulties such as thinking, speaking, remembering, or behaving in the way someone normally would. Dementia comes with both symptoms, which the person experiences, and signs, which others can identify. Although other words may describe changes in memory and thinking, the term dementia is used when these problems have started to change normal daily life routines. The somewhat newer term, major neurocognitive disorder, is used by some as we begin to move toward diagnosing cognitive changes prior to evidence of signs or symptoms.

The face of dementia is changing – slowly but changing. Historically, dementia was diagnosed or acknowledged in the public only at the late stage, when individuals had lost functional and cognitive capacity and were likely eligible for hospice. But with the advent of dementia advocates, as those you are meeting in this book or following on social media, there is much time in dementia to be lived. The time in mild cognitive impairment or early dementia is many years, and with some modifications to lifestyle, may extend even longer (research suggests this is possible). I can imagine that time spent in early-stage dementia will continue to extend. The advocates for living well with dementia will escalate their voices, and dementia will become a long, chronic disease – much like we've seen the changes in cancer over the last 50 years. There are now so many cancer survivors or people living with cancer for extended periods of time. While no one likes to receive a diagnosis of cancer, as no one likes receiving a diagnosis of dementia, most people will have an initial period of grief, then adopt the treatment or lifestyle changes needed, adapt their lives as needed, and live well with a diagnosis.

In the middle stages of dementia, as of the writing of this book, there is time for cognitive and functional loss that requires adapting. During the middle stages, more assistance may be required to live your best life, but there are several strategies that may be helpful. We will discuss them throughout this book.

Many of the exercises and suggestions are to assist in the adapting – exploring and communicating what invigorates you or soothes you, finding what gives your life meaning so that you can inform those who will be assisting you as you move into relying on others for assistance.

Also, as of the writing of this book, there is no cure for dementia. Research is ongoing, and hopefully breakthroughs will continue to be made. Currently, in the last stage, there is a need for total assistance for function and decision-making. The ability to toilet, speak, walk, and, ultimately, to swallow will be lost. Because decisions must be made in your day-to-day life, the goal of this book is to help you imagine what would make life worthwhile and ensure that it is incorporated into your day-to-day life, even as it comes to its end. Your vision, your values, can be part of how you move from living well with dementia to dying with dementia.

Daniel Gibbs, M.D., is a neurologist who was diagnosed with Alzheimer's dementia in his mid-60s but likely had symptoms starting when he lost his ability to smell at about age 57. His memoir, *A Tattoo on my Brain*, is filled with his impressions of coming to the diagnosis and how he is adapting and adjusting as someone with early-stage disease mixed with his clinical experience as a physician. He was aware he likely was developing dementia due to knowledge of a genetic predisposition, his loss of smell, and some subtle symptoms. He states, "But in truth, I'm lucky to have found what I found when I found it. That has meant all the difference, as it has enabled me to access cutting-edge medicine through clinical trials and other progressive treatment options. And I've made some simple lifestyle choices about diet, exercise, and social and intellectual activity that

THE DISEASE

evidence-based science has found beneficial for brain health and resilience, including for those with Alzheimer's."[19]

One of my favorite insights from Dr. Gibbs is a sentiment I have heard from many people living with dementia: "Despite the advances that support earlier diagnosis and treatment of Alzheimer's, assumptions of helplessness and despair have dominated the public conversation. The same is often true in the medical community. Urged by colleagues, I began writing this book as an expansion of that JAMA Neurology paper published in 2019, to press for change in the medical profession, especially among those physicians on the front lines with patients who might benefit. But there's no reason that, as individuals, we have to wait for institutional change. We can take reasonable, responsible, evidence-based steps to help ourselves."[20]

Well said, Dr. Gibbs! Let's get moving on advocating for ourselves!

Why Get A Diagnosis

There are often stories of people having difficulty with changes in their memory, personality. or other symptoms that were ignored or dismissed by a physician. The accurate diagnosis and the process of diagnosing cognitive loss is not perfect and may take time to uncover. If you feel there is something wrong, keep advocating for yourself.

Dr. Gibbs points out that many times we want to ignore or dismiss getting a diagnosis. He states, "That thrill of discovery is not the case for most patients. More often it's a sobering, or

---

[19] Gibbs, Daniel; Barker, Teresa H.. A Tattoo on my Brain (pp. 1-2). Cambridge University Press. Kindle Edition

[20] Gibbs, Daniel; Barker, Teresa H.. A Tattoo on my Brain (p. 7). Cambridge University Press. Kindle Edition.

sometimes frightening, epiphany. Among my patients, reviewing the results of tests and scans that confirmed signs of Alzheimer's got mixed reviews. Some said the information was clarifying: they weren't happy to hear it, but it helped ground their thinking about next steps in a treatment plan we would develop together. Others who came to see me were there at the urging of someone else – sometimes a family member, friend, or perhaps a supervisor at work – and often what they wanted most of all was to avoid a formal diagnosis of dementia. In some cases, they feared losing their job and livelihood. In others, the specter of a dementia diagnosis threatened to upend their sense of themselves and their standing in their profession, family, or community. The positive potential of any treatment was often overshadowed by their fears. The problem in the past was that we didn't recognize the disease until people were already in the moderate to late stages of it. It didn't help that, back when I first started practicing in the early 1990s, there was nothing we could do. There were no drugs, we didn't know anything about lifestyle changes – and I hated that we were so helpless to do anything about it. It was the same as cancer had been twenty years before that. Nobody talked about it. Many people didn't want to know."[21]

As Dr. Gibbs points out, the evaluation process may take time to sort out, and the results may be difficult to face. Positive actions such as lifestyle changes, adopting treatments such as medication (if appropriate), treatment for sleep apnea, and taking time to prepare for communication changes and

---

[21] Gibbs, Daniel; Barker, Teresa H.. A Tattoo on my Brain (p. 85-6). Cambridge University Press. Kindle Edition.

discovery to ease your later stages can help as you face your fears and the potential "upending of your sense of self."

Finally, Dr. Gibbs notes that by facing the difficulty of the diagnosis, you begin to focus more on living. Acknowledging that you have a finite time to make an impact, enjoy your life, gather and give love, makes each day more meaningful.

"In the most universal sense, a diagnosis of Alzheimer's disease is clarifying; it presents the uninvited opportunity to confront your own mortality and get serious about making the most of the time you have. In concrete terms, the sooner you know a disease process has begun, the sooner you can take reasonable steps to stop or slow that process and review your other life."[22]

What is Included in an Evaluation

The tools to diagnose dementia are improving, but making a clear diagnosis can still be difficult. Physicians rely on your history and a physical examination. Questions will be focused on what aspects of your life you are noticing difficulties. You can prepare for this by understanding what the physician may be looking for and having notes ready.

Dr. Gibbs was noticing more slips in his cognitive self, and wanted to catch them so that he could enter a clinical trial. He **prepared** for his physician to find his memory loss. Imagine that! "I stepped up the notetaking on myself, but then realized, when I'd go to review them, that gaps in the entries meant that I sometimes forgot to make any entries at all. Note to self: remember to remember to make notes to self."[23]

---

[22] Gibbs, Daniel; Barker, Teresa H., A Tattoo on my Brain (p. 2). Cambridge University Press. Kindle Edition

[23] Gibbs, Daniel; Barker, Teresa H.. A Tattoo on my Brain (p. 71). Cambridge University Press. Kindle Edition.

The History

In an article by leading dementia specialists, they recommend that physicians complete a systematic set of questions that will encompass all domains of cognitive function. The list of questions is included in Table 1 for your review. You may need to discuss some of these questions with family and friends to understand if others are noticing changes that you may not be as aware of.[24]

Table 1: Targeted Questions to Address Cognitive Domains

Memory	Do you forget appointments or have difficulty keeping track of the day or time? Do you repeat questions or comments? Do you forget recent events or conversations?
Attention	Do you have periods of decreased alertness? Are you easily distracted?
Language	Do you have word-finding difficulties? Struggle to find common words? Do you have trouble communicating thoughts or understanding what is being said?
Visuospatial processing	Do you tend to get lost or turned around? Do you ever fail to see something that is right in front of you?

---

24 (https://www.ncbi.nlm.nih.gov/pmc/articles/PMC7416715/)

Executive function	Can you successfully complete tasks that require multiple steps; for example, planning a trip or throwing a dinner party? Can you use appliances and devices as well as you used to?
Social comportment	Do you behave appropriately in social situations? Does your family agree? Have you become impulsive, careless, or unguarded? Does your family agree?
Adapted from	https://www.ncbi.nlm.nih.gov/pmc/articles/PMC7416715/

Instrumental activities of daily living (IADL) are often where difficulties may arise. The major domains of IADLs include cooking, cleaning, transportation, laundry, and managing finance. While the questions in the table above or reports of difficulty in any of the instrumental activities of daily living may not be completely sensitive to change in cognitive capabilities, they do highlight when cognitive changes impair the function that makes living independently possible and will highlight areas where support can be directed and targeted. Changes in activities of daily living (ADL) include toileting, personal hygiene, continence, dressing, feeding, ambulating may also be occurring, though usually presenting later in the disease process, and may interfere with independent functioning as well.

To prepare for the evaluation by your physician, evaluate these aspects of your life to assist your physician in guiding your cognitive evaluation.

- Managing your budget, including using the ATM, writing checks, and remembering your bills, making unwise purchases, falling prey to telemarketer and scams.
- Managing doctors' appointments, and taking your medications as prescribed
- Planning and preparing nutritious meals
- Being able to do housework and prepare your meals
- Doing your own shopping – groceries, clothing, or anything else you need
- Using the telephone, cell phone, and computer as a means of communication
- Managing transportation – driving, summoning and paying for hired rides (Uber, cabs, Lyft), taking public transportation
- Managing your household in its entirety – including pet care if you have any pets
- Any and all extracurricular activities – maintaining a hobby, socializing with friends, family, and peers, religious organizations, clubs, service organizations, etc.

Changes in IADL may be impaired by other conditions (loss of sight, arthritis), but when living with dementia, we tend to minimize our difficulties and think we are successfully accomplishing more than is evident. This is not a character flaw, but a part of the dementia's impact on thinking. For this reason, I recommend taking an inventory of your abilities and asking family to give you input on how they see your function. Then compare the lists to see where they agree and disagree with you. If family or friends see a deficit that you are not seeing, look for or ask for evidence of this deficit. It is from this place of curiosity and willingness to learn, that an adaptation can be found to make your life run more smoothly.

The physician will also be asking about sleeping patterns. Is there evidence of snoring or disturbed sleep? Sleep disturbance from sleep apnea can adversely affect cognitive function. If you snore, fall asleep easily while sitting (to read, watch television, or when driving), or have morning headaches, it is worth undergoing a sleep study (called a polysomnogram). The evidence that treating sleep apnea will benefit cognition is strong and should be followed up to preserve brain function.

Evidence of nightmares, restless leg syndrome, and acting out your dreams (rapid eye movement sleep disorder) have been linked to certain types of cognitive loss. Rapid eye movement (REM) sleep behavior disorder is a sleep disorder in which you physically act out vivid, often unpleasant, dreams with vocal sounds and sudden, often violent, arm and leg movements during REM sleep – sometimes called dream-enacting behavior. If you have these symptoms, please let your physician know.

A down mood can worsen cognitive function or could be caused by the changes in the brain from the cognitive alterations. Because neuropsychiatric symptoms can both cause and be caused by mood disorders and neurodegenerative diseases, it's important to discuss them openly. On the initial appointment, the physician may not bring up any symptoms like this, trying to balance gaining your trust and comfort while teasing through the options that may be causing cognitive difficulties. Knowing this, be prepared to report any symptoms that you feel may be contributing, the most common being feeling blue, feeling stress, or losing the desire to do much of anything (apathy). Also consider reporting other odd occurrences if you are experiencing them such as seeing things that others do not or feeling that people are against you. For example, people with dementia who also have Lewy body disease often experience anxiety, delusions, and visual hallucinations.

Realize that depression is very common in the first year after diagnosis, as adapting to the diagnosis will take time and processing. Dr. Gibbs describes beautifully what I have heard from several patients. He says, "An early spring check-up with Dr. Rabinovici, my neurologist at UCSF, surprisingly showed my cognitive testing was unchanged from the year before. He noted one change: I scored high on the depression evaluation, which didn't surprise me at all. Virtually everyone who receives a diagnosis of Alzheimer's disease will suffer what doctors call reactive, or situational, depression. The diagnosis is, on the face of it, depressing. It's tough news to get. The future appears bleak. There is a real sense of loss. There is grieving. Even though I didn't yet have that diagnosis, I'm a neurologist, after all, and I knew what I knew: it was coming. My answers on the depression evaluation stated the obvious: Did I feel sad? Of course, I felt sad. Did I feel discouraged about the future? Of course, I did, particularly given that I knew about studies underway that might slow the progress of this disease in its early stages, but my cognitive impairment wasn't 'bad enough' to qualify for them. So, I was witnessing my own neurodegeneration in slow motion, and adding to my frustration was the fact that the debate about how to formally classify or even identify early-stage Alzheimer's stood between me and potential new treatments."[25]

The doctor will also ask about a few miscellaneous items that may be linked to cognitive concerns that include occupational or recreational head trauma, loss of smell, any difficulty with walking, falls, tremors, loss of ability to control bowels or bladder, and any difficulty with swallowing (such as coughing during eating). The doctor should ask about factors in your social situation that may affect thinking such as illicit drug use, problematic alcohol or marijuana use, and social stressors. The physician will be asking whether family members have known memory or cognitive difficulties. Additionally, the physician should review all your medications, noting drugs that contribute to cognitive decline, especially anticholinergic drugs (e.g., diphenhydramine [Benadryl]; doxylamine [Unisom]).

The Examination

The examination will also include a physical examination assessing neurologic signs, specifically looking for changes in how your eyes, mouth, speaking, and walking may be affected (or not).

There will be a brief mental status screen often using a standardized tool. There may be a standardized tool to assess your mood as well. These tests take only about 3-10 minutes and cannot definitively diagnose cognitive loss but will guide the physician on what more should be done.

---

[25] Gibbs, Daniel; Barker, Teresa H.. A Tattoo on my Brain (p. 76). Cambridge University Press. Kindle Edition

Testing That May Be Done

Laboratory testing: Blood work will be done to screen for conditions that may contribute to memory loss or cognitive dysfunction, such as vitamin deficiencies, thyroid abnormalities, some infectious causes (syphilis, HIV), and electrolyte and metabolic imbalances. More extensive testing, such as genetic testing, would not be done at this early stage of evaluation.

Brain Imaging: In most individuals, the physician will obtain some type of brain imaging – either a computed tomography scan (CT or CAT scan) or a magnetic resonance imaging (MRI). The physician will be looking for the uncommon tumor, evidence of stroke, mini-strokes or vascular issues, and any changes in areas of the brain that can signify excess brain tissue loss in one area over another.

Sleep study: I believe most people should have a screening sleep study. The evidence that altered sleep can contribute to cognitive loss is solid, and not all people who have altered sleep also snore. The treatment is is without side effects and can be incorporated into your daily routine, though may take some effort (cleaning) and getting used to.

Referral for neuropsychologic testing: If there is a question as to whether something like depression is complicating interpretation the simple cognitive testing, more extensive neuropsychological testing can be very helpful. More detailed testing may show weaknesses (and strengths) that less comprehensive tests miss. By examining patterns of cognition, neuropsychologists also help diagnose underlying causes of deficits and areas of strength that can be used in adapting to the cognitive loss.

What Can a Specialist Offer?

There are several reasons to see a dementia specialist (a neurologist or geriatrician that specializes in dementia; there are national specialty centers housed in large academic centers). The first and likely most important point to consider is if you are not satisfied with the diagnosis and feel a specialist can assist in fine-tuning the diagnosis and therefore the approach.

Characteristics of dementia that may warrant seeing a specialist would be early onset, rapid progression, or atypical presentation. The specialist may go even further, clarifying testing. That may include genetic testing. Further brain imaging may include a fluorodeoxyglucose-PET scan of the brain that can distinguish between frontotemporal dementia (FTD) and Alzheimer's disease (AD).

A lumbar puncture may be required to obtain cerebrospinal fluid to test for markers of several types of dementia or non-dementia causes for cognitive changes (such as infections, autoimmune disorders, or cancers).

Finally, a specialist will often have clinical trials that may be of interest and offer access to an amyloid PET scan (which is not covered by insurance).

Why consider a clinical trial? It's true that a clinical trial may not help you personally, but it likely is the way that a cure for dementia will be found! When you are involved in a clinical trial, you will often receive very personal care by some of the nation's leading dementia specialists. Volunteers often find the experience to be interesting and gratifying, but it is not for everyone.

Here are some thoughts by Dr. Gibbs on his participation in several clinical trials. "The fact that I have no illusions that I will directly benefit from any of these trials isn't remarkable – I'm a scientist and that's just how I think. For me, what's exciting is the opportunity to contribute to research as a volunteer participant, for a change, instead of as the clinician, or as the research scientist I'd been so many years earlier. That gave me a sense of purpose and still does. I recognize that the chance of me personally benefiting from a study, in terms of prolonging my life or slowing progression of my Alzheimer's, is very small. What I hope is that my participation will benefit the next generation, my children's generation, so that Alzheimer's becomes a controllable disease within their lifetime, if not within mine. From a personal point of view, it's for my children. That's how I put a face on it. They're at increased risk and I would do anything to help find something to help so it's not an issue for them when they get older. No breakthrough. No magic bullet. But perhaps a block in that pyramid."[26]

Brief Overview of Each Type of Dementia

There are likely hundreds of types of dementia, and in time, understanding them will lead us to better treatments. We are in a time when nuances and new genetic variants of cognitive loss are being found and further investigated. This is good news; as we discover differences in dementia, the research on what is helpful for some and not others will refine our treatment choices and improve the medical approach to dementia. Similarly, the non-pharmacologic approach can also differ depending on the type of dementia that is present.

---

26 Gibbs, Daniel; Barker, Teresa H.. A Tattoo on my Brain (p. 119). Cambridge University Press. Kindle Edition.

The changes that take place in brain cells and deeper within the brain helps us better understand what sort of dementia has developed. Each area of the brain is responsible for certain tasks or functions. When areas are damaged, the corresponding pattern of behavioral and mental issues aids in determining the diagnosis. There can be more than one type of dementia developing as well, so an individual may have both Alzheimer's dementia and vascular dementia, for example.

Alzheimer's dementia: Alzheimer's disease is the most common cause of dementia, representing at least 70 percent of all persons with dementia and affecting approximately 15 percent of all people over 65 years of age. The cause of Alzheimer's disease remains unclear, but there are proteins (amyloid and tau) that form plaques and neurofibrillary tangles in the brain that are thought to be impairing neural cell function.

The symptoms often begin with memory loss, but some variants begin with difficulty with executive function, language, or visuospatial symptoms. Memory loss may present as complaints of items being lost, missing appointments or medications, or repeating stories.

Dementia with Lewy body (DLB): DLB is the second most common form of dementia and is characterized by clumps in the brain from alpha-synuclein, another neural protein. The deposits are the same as seen in Parkinson's disease but occur in different regions of the brain. DLB is a combination of physical symptoms (difficulty with gait, tremors, slowness) and cognitive symptoms (memory, executive function, and prominent visuospatial difficulty) with a hallmark that some days can be very good and others very bad – a feature known as fluctuations.

Finally, there are often hallucinations and characteristic sleep disturbances (rapid eye movement sleep disorder).

Frontotemporal dementia (FTD): FTD includes a host of dementias that are clustered under this title. There is a motor presentation, a language presentation, and a behavioral presentation. FTD represents approximately 5 percent of dementias. Behavioral symptoms are changes in attention, problems organizing, and personality changes. Language issues usually present as a non-fluent aphasia that develops over months or years. The motor symptoms may be similar to Parkinson's disease.

Vascular dementia: Vascular dementia is a term used to describe cognitive issues, such as difficulties in reasoning, planning, memory, and judgment. This type of dementia results from blocked arteries within the brain, which can be caused by a stroke. However, not all strokes result in vascular dementia; it depends on where the stroke occurs and how severe it is. Likewise, other conditions that impair blood flow to your brain may lead to this form of dementia due to an inadequate supply of oxygen and nutrients being delivered throughout your body.

There are several other types of dementia that we will not review here. The purpose of this book is not to provide an exhaustive overview of each type of dementia, but I will provided a brief overview of the five most common types of dementia. For a more comprehensive and up-to-date review, consider *Navigating Life with Dementia* by James Noble, MD, MD, CPH, FAAN, Associate Professor of Neurology, The Taub Institute for Research on Alzheimer's Disease and the Aging Brain.

What Recommendations Work to Keep Dementia at Bay?

There is ample research that life choices are important to slow or prevent cognitive loss. I would like to begin with the following recommendations. These recommendations have the most scientific backing, keep the entire body (mind, body, spirit) healthy and working in top condition. This helps to preserve cognitive function, and protect the brain from inflammation, stress, abnormal changes in hormones, and enhance spiritual expansion. Medications, on the other hand, have limited benefits and accompanying side effects. I pray that you adopt as many changes into your life as you can, to take agency of your health.

"We all know that Alzheimer's robs us of the future we hoped for. But, in the absence of attention to the risk factors, at this earliest stage of the disease and the potential for positive interventions, our silence allows Alzheimer's to rob us of even more – possibly years more."[27]

Dr. Gibbs, as always, gets right to the heart of things.

Exercise: Numerous research studies have demonstrated that exercise regimens can improve or maintain not only the functional well-being of those with dementia, but also their cognitive capacity. The dose should be moderate aerobic exercise for approximately 180 minutes per week. Exercise can be broken into shorter bursts or longer periods – whatever works for you. Exercise can be done in a group setting (walk with a friend, dance with a group, take a class). Group exercise adds a social element which is also beneficial. Mindfulness-based

---

[27] Gibbs, Daniel; Barker, Teresa H.. A Tattoo on my Brain (p. 180). Cambridge University Press. Kindle Edition

exercise combines the benefits of mindfulness with exercise and has been shown to be especially beneficial to those with mild cognitive impairment (MCI) or early-stage disease.

"Lately, although I've started to notice some decline in cognition, more forgetfulness and befuddlement, I still think more clearly during and after exercise. This has been borne out in this study so far. On average, my cognitive assessment score increases 8 percent after aerobic exercise. Today, my fitness tracker says my heart rate is 131, up from a baseline of 64 at the start of the hike. After the 1.75-mile, 57-minute hike from the boat dock to the top of Beacon Rock, elevation gain 850 feet, the cognitive assessment score has increased by 15 percent."[28]

Mindfulness: We know that mindfulness has been shown to be beneficial to mental health, reducing stress and improving depression, but a recent compilation of several studies shows that mindfulness practice can also improve executive function, the aspect of cognition that assists in the ability to live independently.[29]

Cognitive Reserve and Cognitive Stimulation Therapy: Cognitive reserve is defined as "the ability to optimize or maximize performance through differential recruitment of brain networks."[30] The concept of cognitive reserve was proposed to explain why some individuals with considerable brain damage/

---

28   Gibbs, Daniel; Barker, Teresa H.. A Tattoo on my Brain (p. 18). Cambridge University Press. Kindle Edition.
29   T. Whitfield *et al*. The Effect of Mindfulness-based Programs on Cognitive Function in Adults: A Systematic Review and Meta-analysis. *Neuropsychol Rev*, published online August 4, 2021; doi: 10.1007/s11065-021-09519-y
30   Stern Y. Cognitive reserve in ageing and Alzheimer's disease. Lancet Neurology 2012; 11: 1006–1012; https://doi.org/10.1016/S1474-4422(12)70191-96 (public access version available at www.ncbi.nlm.nih.gov/pmc/articles/PMC3507991

pathology still have no visible symptoms. Scientists hypothesize that cognitive reserve results from a combination of an increased number and connection of neurons in the brain, developed from a lifetime of intellectually stimulating experiences. If some brain cells are lost due to cognitive loss, the connected neurons previously developed will find a new path to compensate for the loss. This allows for reserved function even in the face of early brain cell loss.

"While nothing has proved reliably effective in clinical trials so far, a lot has been learned about what goes on in the brain during the disease process. The role of cognitive reserve and resiliency is something of a wild card – it's not fully understood – but it is emerging as a promising factor in the brain's capacity to forestall the effects of Alzheimer's for a longer period without significant symptoms. For those of us with early-stage Alzheimer's, it may offer a potential reprieve from the otherwise steady erosion of our faculties by the neurodegenerative disease process."[31]

With this thought of Dr. Gibbs in mind, there has been a program, Aimee Spector, PhD, Senior Lecturer at the University of London, developed called Cognitive Stimulation Therapy. (CST) It has been shown to consistently improve cognitive function for people with dementia and is associated with improved quality of life and communication. These benefits are equal to those found with medication and are additive to the benefits of medicine when used together. CST is an 8-week program that guides people through a series of themed activities designed to promote continued learning so that they can stay mentally

---

[31] Gibbs, Daniel; Barker, Teresa H.. A Tattoo on my Brain (p. 89). Cambridge University Press. Kindle Edition.

stimulated and socially engaged. Activities may include puzzles or games, playing instruments, or engaging in conversation with other group members and/or program facilitators with focus on building strengths, offering opinions (rather than memory-based facts) and enhancing self-confidence. Because social engagement is a key component of CST, the intervention is most often administered in a group setting. It is worthwhile finding a cognitive stimulation therapy program offered near you, or you can inquire with the Alzheimer's Association if a program could be started near you.

Nutrition: While it seems trite to mention nutrition, it has a significant impact on cognitive function. First, avoiding food and drinks that may be toxic to the brain should be encouraged. The use of alcohol may need to be limited to none if there is evidence of poor effects on brain function, and low or moderate use otherwise. Food that does not adversely affect overall health should be chosen, so there is a recommendation to avoid fried and processed foods. There is good evidence that the Mediterranean diet is beneficial to cognitive function, specifically that those with MCI are less likely to convert to a diagnosis of dementia when following the Mediterranean diet.

Social Engagement: Loneliness is associated with increased risk of depression and dementia. Therefore, avoiding or actively working to limit loneliness is paramount. Evidence reveals that active community cultural engagement, such as visiting museums and attending the theater, may serve as a protective measure against the risk of dementia. Social engagement is invigorating when it includes individuals from beyond your closest circle. Change it up! Expand your network. Ask new people or join a programmed event where you may meet new people.

<u>Sleep</u>: Primarily following the recommendations for good sleep hygiene sounds fancy, but it is just adopting good sleep habits.

Good sleep hygiene is all about putting yourself in the best position to sleep well each and every night. Or day, if you work on opposite schedule! Optimizing your sleep schedule, pre-bed routine, and daily routines are part of harnessing habits to make quality sleep feel more automatic. At the same time, creating a pleasant bedroom environment can be an invitation to relax and doze off.

Set a sleep schedule. Having a fixed bedtime/wake-up time puts you into a rhythm of consistent sleep. To develop this habit, gradually move your bedtime to the new time. If you nap in the day, limit naps to 20 minutes to allow sleep at night and avoid deep sleep in the day.

Follow a nightly routine. Change into night clothes, brush your teeth, turn off electronics at least 30-60 minutes prior to bed (to avoid the blue light that interferes with melatonin – the sleep hormone), dim the lights, use relaxation techniques such as meditation, calming music, rhythmic breathing, body scans, and/or progressive muscle relaxation to facilitate onset of sleep. If you do not fall asleep within 20 minutes, do not linger in bed. Get up to stretch or read until you feel sleepy and then return to bed. Beds are not for tossing and turning – only sleep.

Optimize your bedroom for sleep. Are your mattress and pillow comfortable? Do you find your bedding comfortable? Keep the temperature on the cool side (e.g., 65 degrees F). Limit light and noise interruption. An eye mask and a white noise machine may help. Some find a lavender pillow spray or other light smells facilitate a calming environment. This may include a sleep partner who snores or hogs your bedding. Adjust the environment to maximize your sleep.

Other habits that promote sleep include limiting caffeine in the afternoon or evening; avoiding late, heavy meals; and minimizing alcohol intake, especially later in the evening.

<u>Medications</u>: Maximize treatment for anything that can be contributory to cognitive decline.

If the cognitive impairment is being caused by an underlying condition, that should be treated first and foremost. If you've been found to have hypothyroidism, for example, that should be treated, and medications adjusted until the appropriate dose is found. If you have sleep apnea, obtaining and adjusting to continuous positive airway pressure (CPAP) to alleviate that condition. Other risk factors for cognitive decline, like hypertension, diabetes, and smoking, should also be addressed. And finally, any medications known to cause cognitive impairment – particularly anticholinergic drugs – should be reduced or stopped if possible. A list of common anti-cholinergic medications can be found at the Mayo Clinic website.[32]

<u>Medication Specifically for Dementia</u>: As of the writing of this book, there are no approved therapies known to stop or reverse the effects of neurodegenerative disorders. There are potential treatments in clinical trials, but the only medications currently available offer symptomatic relief. It is important to know which type of dementia is being treated. Some treatments will not help some types of dementia (and therefore could cause harm due to side effects in the face of no benefit) or may worsen the underlying symptoms.

---

[32] https://www.mayoclinic.org/drugs-supplements/anticholinergics-and-antispasmodics-oral-route-parenteral-route-rectal-route-transdermal-route/description/drg-20070312.

Acetylcholinesterase inhibitor therapy works to better or maintain memory and concentration by blocking the destruction of acetylcholine, a neurotransmitter. Acetylcholinesterase inhibitors (AChEIs) such as donepezil, galantamine, and rivastigmine may improve symptoms in patients with AD dementia, vascular dementia, and DLB, but may worsen behavior in FTD. There is no strong evidence that AChEIs are beneficial for those with MCI. In fact, the beneficial effects are minimal such that if side effects are present, the medicine should likely be discontinued. Side effects include nausea, gastrointestinal distress, diarrhea, slowed heart rate, leg cramps and disturbing dreams.

Memantine, an N-methyl-D-aspartate or NMDA receptor antagonist, is believed to be effective by blocking excess glutamate and stimulating the expression of NMDA receptors. It has been approved for use in moderate to severe Alzheimer's disease (AD) and is commonly used, off-label, for mild to moderate vascular dementia. It is found to have modest improvements in thinking, everyday functioning, behavior, and mood. Side effects are few; dizziness is the most common one.

Aducanumab and lecanemab-irmb are monoclonal antibody medications that targets aggregated forms of amyloid beta found in the brains of people with Alzheimer's disease to reduce its buildup. It is only approved for individuals with mild cognitive impairment or early-stage Alzheimer's disease. While it is approved due to its ability to lessen amyloid plaques as evident on brain scans, it has not been shown to improve daily function, thinking, or memory.

Furthermore, the use and approval are controversial due to the extensive side effects that include amyloid-related imaging abnormalities-edema (ARIA-E), in which the brain swells;

amyloid-related imaging abnormalities-hemosiderin deposition (ARIA-H), which includes small brain bleeds (microhemorrhage); and brain bleeding along the surface of the brain (superficial siderosis). The long-term effects of these imaging changes are not known due to the limited number of people in studies thus far and the limited time for follow-up. Use is currently limited as the treatment is very expensive, and time- and labor-intensive. Medicare has recently decided it is eligible for coverage, but many physicians are not sure the benefits outweigh the significant risks.

In conclusion of this section, the words of Dr. Gibbs again resonate.

"As mindful choices, mindful acts, they help provide structure to my thoughts and actions, hope for the future, and a greater sense of happiness and well-being that feels realistic, not merely optimistic. Taking charge, having a sense of being at least to some degree in control, can be an antidote to hopelessness and depression. As close to a prescription as you can get, the five main anti-Alzheimer's strategies are: (1) aerobic exercise; (2) a Mediterranean-style, or the MIND, diet; (3) mentally stimulating activity; (4) social engagement; and (5) good sleep, along with good control of diabetes and high blood pressure, if present. Admittedly, these have become such familiar recommendations for a generally healthy lifestyle that they are practically a cliché. It would be easy to shrug them off and put them off for a later time. But for someone with Alzheimer's, or with a strong genetic risk for it, 'later' is a gamble. Sooner is the better bet. These strategies have been shown to be most effective in slowing the disease process in the early stages of cell-level changes – the ten to twenty years before significant cognitive impairment. Especially for someone with early-stage Alzheimer's or a significant risk of developing Alzheimer's, this is vital time in your favor. It has been for me."[33]

Points to Remember

- The face of dementia is changing – we no longer only consider the latest stage but are understanding that dementia can be a chronic condition that we live with well, accommodate, and adapt to, and, hopefully, prepare for the phase when we begin to die from the disease.
- The earlier you can confirm your diagnosis and the type of dementia you are living with, the better the chance you can adopt lifestyle changes, explore clinical trials, and begin medications (or avoid them) for your best current life.
- The evaluation for dementia can be complicated. Be prepared with answers to frequently needed information to facilitate an accurate diagnosis.
- As dementia may not present in a straightforward way, the diagnosis may be missed or partial early in the disease. Continue to advocate for direct answers.
- An accurate diagnosis may require the expertise of a specialist. Characteristics of dementia that may warrant seeing a specialist would be early onset, rapid progression, or atypical presentation. Discuss whether any medical conditions or medications need attention and whether medications or research could benefit your cognitive status.

---

[33] Gibbs, Daniel; Barker, Teresa H.. A Tattoo on my Brain (p. 126). Cambridge University Press. Kindle Edition.

- There are several lifestyle options that may prevent or help with cognitive decline including the Mediterranean diet, exercise, socialization, cognitive reserve (and cognitive stimulation therapy), mindfulness, and attention to sleep hygiene and/or sleep issues.

Action Plan

- Understand what type of dementia you have so that you can best prepare for the adaptations that will be likely needed to live well.
- Be sure to schedule an appointment with your primary physician or a dementia specialist to confirm your diagnosis, ensure that reversible factors in cognitive loss are adequately managed, and address depression (a common initial reaction to the diagnosis).
- If you feel you are not satisfied with the level of information or evaluation you've received, consider making an appointment with a dementia specialist to augment your care.
- Evaluate your lifestyle choices from the perspective of brain health – are there any areas that can be augmented? Adopt more fruits and vegetables and less processed foods in your diet, walk for aerobic exercise, expand your social circle by inviting new friends to engage in interesting activities, and ensure that you do not have sleep apnea.

Resources

Daniel Gibbs and Teresa H. Barker, A Tattoo on my Brain: A Neurologist's Personal Battle against Alzheimer's Disease.

This is a first-person memoir written by Dr. Daniel Gibbs. Dr. Gibbs is a neurologist, teacher, and researcher that suspected he may have Alzheimer's dementia due to genetic testing. His memoir combines his knowledge of dementia from his perspective as a physician working with individuals living with dementia and as a patient. He candidly describes waiting for the diagnosis while managing lifestyle changes to minimize the impact of the cognitive loss and the psychological wranglings of dealing with the diagnosis.

Gayatri Devi, The Spectrum of Hope: An Optimistic and New Approach to Alzheimer's Disease and other Dementias.

A Spectrum of Hope is a very insightful book about the treatment and new approaches to dealing with Alzheimer's disease and other dementias. The author Gayatri Devi, M.D., is a neurologist and she specializes in dementia.

Devi provides important information for patients and caregivers. In the book she uses stories about her patients to help paint a picture of how she approaches and manages the dementia diagnosis along with her patients and caregivers.

Chapter 3

STIGMA

The Kenny Family Story

My mom was a "joiner." She volunteered throughout her life for several organizations, even though she worked full-time from the time her children were all in school until she met retirement age. Retirement for her was a time for more activities. She was the morning receptionist for the church we attended, she was an usher for the orchestra, and she trained to be a clown and visited skilled nursing facilities to bring some joy and surprise to many who lived there. Her social life included lunches, parties, and dinners with friends from her child-rearing days, couples (or singles via death or divorce) that she prayed or traveled with, or those she worked with. Widowed in her early fifties, she had built a multi-generational network to meet her extroverted social needs. She had known what it was like to be uncomfortable in social situations during that time in her early widowhood. "It is so hard being the third wheel," she would lament as she put the finishing touches on her make-up or while waiting at the door for a ride to a party. Her body would be a bit shrunken as she would go out the door. Several hours later, she would dance through the door, smiling face, shine in her eyes. "I had such a good time! Brenda was telling us stories of her trip to Africa. I need to plan a safari trip."

I would laugh at her renewed energy and ask, "I guess it's not that bad being the third wheel?"

"Oh, it's bad," she would say. "But the rewards are worth it!" My mom knew herself, her need for social interaction and had the courage to push her feelings of awkwardness aside to fill her deeper need. This trait was honed and ready when her organizational skills were lapsing during her early stages of dementia. She was used to accepting rides from others, being the "third wheel," being in uncomfortable situations. Don't get me wrong—she didn't want to give up driving when the time came that she could no longer do so safely, nor did she enjoy when someone she loved spending time with failed to return calls because she was repeating herself and some stories. All those things hurt, and she grieved them. But she wasn't stopped. She pushed through her discomfort. She moved to assisted living to allow her to enhance the fulfillment for social connections. This worked well for some time, but as her disease progressed, she was unable to participate in the pottery, current events, and walking programs as she did before. The individuals at the facility began to limit their time with my mother due to her changing conversational capacity and missing social cues. Activities and socialization were still important to her, but she needed more structure and support. The facility had an on-site day program for individuals living with dementia in the community. My sister suggested she volunteer there to allow her to accept the transition to the day program with more grace. She arranged that idea with the day program (though, in fact, my mother would be a participant), bought my mother new easy-to-assemble outfits, and arranged an escort to the day program. My mother began to "volunteer" there and to thrive again, with the structure and socialization in her life.

What do we know about stigma? Why is it there? There is stigma around the diagnosis of several medical conditions: any or most mental health conditions, AIDS/HIV, addictions, and Alzheimer's disease. There is also stigma around talking about several subjects: gender discrimination, salary, and death.

This book deals with two stigmas: the diagnosis of Alzheimer's dementia and speaking about death. We need to deal with both to move forward. We need to understand what gets in the way of dealing with the issues ourselves and in those we encounter whether family, friends, or healthcare workers.

We must not forget ageism either. Mary Pipher, cultural anthropologist, psychologist, and author of Women Rowing North, speaks of ageism in her book. She describes a Yale School of Public Health study that reveals 75 percent of young people denigrate older adults on Facebook. Pipher uses this study to highlight that there is no "cultural script" for stories of "our complexity, our wisdom and our joy," and that this isn't true in every culture. In the U.S., we are in a culture that values independence, and we see ourselves in this culture as either independent or dependent, never both. In fact, as Pipher posits, we are all **always** interdependent. She suggests that if we could see ourselves this way, we could "reconceptualize the interactions between the young and old. Young people would be more appreciative of what we have to offer. Older people could see themselves as part of a circle of caring that begins with our oldest living relatives and flows down to the youngest baby." When we don't interact, we stereotype. "When we interact, we understand our interconnectedness and value each other's gifts."

Pipher's work reminds us to challenge our own ageism and develop interconnectedness across generations. We need to begin to fight our isolation. As a nation, we value independence, but an unfortunate outcome is isolation. That is not a value that enhances our well-being.

Kate Swaffer's Remarks on Stigma

Kate Swaffer, an advocate for persons living with dementia and someone who herself lives with dementia, often says there is so much discussion about people with dementia without them being part of the conversation. And she reports, if this is so, the stigma will not end. The role of stigma includes "being negatively labelled a loss of status and power, discrimination and stereotyping. Stigma affects a number of things when considering dementia, including the person's willingness to seek diagnosis, to seek support once diagnosed, and a lack of willingness to participate in research."[34]

When individuals are interviewed about what they think about people living with dementia, reported responses are that PLWD cannot participate in meaningful conversations (50 percent of people surveyed), can be irritating (30 percent of people surveyed), and have poor personal hygiene (14 percent of

---

34 Swaffer, Kate. What the Hell Happened to My Brain. Chapter 18, page 191-192.

people surveyed).[35] It is likely most of us think these things and you may have these thoughts about dementia yourself. Richard Taylor speaks about the biases he notices of others and finishes with his own difficulty in finding himself, acknowledging his own dementia bias.[36] The diagnosis of dementia puts us face-to-face with our own prejudices. Can we face those demons? Can we address our own prejudices in order to accept our diagnosis and challenge the prejudices? Can we potentially learn a new way to see our dementia so that we can grow and thrive while living with a disease most do not want to accept?

Facing Our Fears and Our Prejudices

Holly's Story

Holly was a "put together" woman; her hair was tinted blue; her clothes were pressed and pristine. She was proud of her education at an all-women New England college and mentioned her role in her now-deceased husband's business success. "Dr. Kenny, can we test my cognition? I feel like I'm slipping at my bridge game. I need to know I'm not developing dementia. It is the only thing I couldn't endure; I refuse to be near the people at the senior center who are not of right mind. It is why I will only participate in the bridge game." Holly continued, "My bridge partners are always inviting me to their multi-media art sessions, but I don't find the sessions intellectually stimulating enough." Her cognitive screen revealed an inability to remember one of three objects but was otherwise unremarkable. She completed neuropsychological testing and was found

---

[35] Phillipson L, Magee C, Jones S, Skladzien E. Correlates off dementia attitudes in a sample of middle-aged Australian adults. Australian J Aging 2012; 33:158-163.
[36] Richard Taylor, Ph.D., *Alzheimer's from the Inside Out* (2007). p. 153.

to have scores consistent with a mild cognitive impairment. Holly despaired with this knowledge. She stopped attending her weekly bridge game. She became isolated and her appetite declined, her sleep became disturbed, and she refused to participate in psychotherapy. We met often to support her through her diagnosis. After starting an anti-depressant and biweekly sessions with me for emotional support, Holly started to begin accepting some suggestions for reengaging and adopting some coping strategies. We discussed meeting her bridge partners for coffee after the game. "Dr. Kenny, they are so nice. I have not told them my diagnosis, but that I'm having some medical issues and medication changes limiting my ability to play bridge. They keep urging me to come to the art class with them so we can keep up our friendship." "Why not try it?" I asked. After attending an art class, she mentioned watching people closely and not being sure who had cognitive loss and who did not. "One woman had some beautiful pieces, but when I tried to speak with her, she obviously could not put sentences together – how could she even be out in public?" "Holly, you mentioned how beautiful her art is – what makes her life worthy? Only language?" We continued our discussion of personhood and her fears of and prejudices about dementia. I asked Holly if she would be willing to volunteer at a day-program for individuals living with dementia, as part of her therapy, to assist her in challenging some of her preconceived notions about dementia. She reluctantly agreed. We met again in a few months. "I've learned so much!" she told me. "I fumbled and failed during my first few sessions at the day program. I would ask people questions and become frustrated when they couldn't respond. The staff was patient with me and showed me that I needed to give the people in the program more time to respond. They also modeled how to connect without worrying about what was being said. I finally calmed down – you know, I relax more there than anywhere. I am not as worried about how I feel or look – I just focus on the person in front of me. We enjoy each other. I've made a few friends there!"

Holly faced some of her own fears and prejudices and found that persons living with dementia had much to offer if she gave them a chance. She could then reengage in the world knowing that she, as well, had much to offer. She had friends who missed her – whether she played bridge or not. Holly showed many of the common beliefs typical of people living with early dementia – she held or worried about public expectations that PLWD could not participate in meaningful exchanges and feared being perceived as or feeling stupid. And once she faced her fears, she reframed her condition as "lucky" and appreciative that she had friends, could make new friends, and learned to relax.[37]

New Information on Stigma Informed by Those Living with Dementia

Tia Powell, a psychiatrist and bioethicist, wrote a piece for a Hastings Center Special Report noting that the journey with dementia will be wrought with ups and downs, but that, thus far, media focuses on the extremes, limiting our understanding of the "true" journey and flaming stigmatized public opinion. She quotes Lonni Schicker, who spoke from her lived experience of dementia at the 2017 National Research Summit on Care. Services, and Supports for Persons with Dementia and Their

---

37 Ashworth, R. Perceptions of stigma among people affected by early- and late-onset Alzheimer's disease. J Health Psychol 2017; 0:1-21.

Caregivers, sponsored by the U.S. Department of Health and Human Services. "People are always at a loss for words when I tell them that my oldest friends and some family members have limited or no contact with me since my diagnosis, despite my efforts to stay in contact with them. ... People are afraid of the diagnosis and stay away, whether intentionally or unintentionally, because of the uncomfortableness of it all. Those who are with me are with me, and they no doubt will continue to be. ... We all know that it will only be more intense. ... Decline is inevitable. The obstacles are immense. I have had intense mood swings to the point of suicidal ideation. I fall. I get lost. I don't understand money. I have more health issues. ... I have seen my loving, devoted son cry out of frustration and anticipation of what is to come."[38] The quotes highlight the increasing needs of one living with dementia, and that the need for "peace, comfort, companionship, care" will persist.[39]

In a study that compiled interviews with several individuals living with dementia, participants reported what they would want from relationships – specifically friendships. Positive social interaction is important to personal well-being, providing emotional, psychological, and health benefits. The study's authors used the theory of Social Positioning as a guide in understanding the need for the give-and-take of reciprocal exchanges in relationships, which provide balance and equity. The authors found PLWD share five key themes from their interviews. They value longevity in friendship, helping one another as a normal part of friendship, feeling "alive" through the give-and-take of

---

[38] Powell, T "Tho much is taken, much abides": A Good Life within Dementia. Hastings Center Report 2018; 48(5):S71-74

[39] ibid, pg S74

friendship, knowing that someone is there for them, and seeking security through friendship.[40]

To Disclose or Not to Disclose the Diagnosis

There is a qualitative study by Deborah O'Connor and colleagues that describes a series of interviews that occurred over 16 weeks about disclosure and stigma with several individuals living with dementia. Many participants noted that once they acknowledge their diagnosis with someone, such as a financial advisor or on an application for a volunteer organization, they are no longer considered – they become "invisible." Many described being discerning as to whether they disclose their diagnosis, so as not to limit their ability for personal growth and autonomy. Some in the group, in early interviews meeting, did not identify the actions of others as discriminatory, feeling that they might not have been interpreting those actions correctly. Over the course of the 16 weeks, all "could identify personal situations where someone had responded to their disclosure in ways that could be construed as belittling, discounting and/or devaluing."[41]

Gayatri Devi, MD, neurologist and author of *The Spectrum of Hope*, suggests that when individuals are first diagnosed with dementia, they adopt a "don't tell" policy. She stresses that this is a personal decision and must be tailored to the individual person and their supports, but outlines the following reasons for discernment in sharing your diagnosis: "People

---

[40] Perion, J., & Steiner, V. (2019). Perceptions of reciprocity in friendship by community dwelling people with mild to moderate dementia. Dementia, 18(6), 2107-2121.

[41] O'Connor D, Mann J, Wiersma E. Stigma, discrimination and agency: Diagnostic disclosure as an everyday practice shaping social citizenship. J Aging Stud. 2018 Mar;44:45-51. doi: 10.1016/j.jaging.2018.01.010. Epub 2018 Feb 9. PMID: 29502789. reference

may underestimate your competence and intelligence and treat you in ways you find patronizing; your reactions and decisions may be second-guessed and attributed to dementia, even by well-meaning friends and family; if your friends and family treat you differently, your confidence may diminish and your anxiety level may rise." She finishes with "All that said, telling may be better than dealing with the anxiety of keeping the diagnosis private."[42]

What's to Risk if I Don't Disclose?

These stories remind us that discrimination and stigma run deep. Most don't even realize they hold these beliefs – including those that are living with dementia. We, then, can stigmatize ourselves. I have had several patients tell me they will no longer go to programs at senior centers or card games with friends, as they don't want to acknowledge their changes. I respond that if one needed glasses to see more clearly, one would wear them. Many patients have laughed at me and remind me that many of us won't use glasses, hearing aids, walkers, or go on outings due to fear, pride and embarrassment. I recognize that this may be true. But the "interventions" improve our chance for limiting the progression of the dementia or fighting its potential sequel, depression. Evidence shows that glasses, hearing aids, walkers, and social engagement keep us alert and ward off depression. Isolation and loneliness have recently been linked to several adverse health outcomes, including high blood pressure, Alzheimer's dementia, and depression and anxiety.[43]

---

42 Devi, Gayatri, MD. The Spectrum of Hope. p. 61
43 Cacioppo JT and Cacioppo S. The growing problem of loneliness. **Lancet** 2018;391(10119):426.

Limiting the disclosure of the disease to others may be necessary to continue living your life to the fullest for some time. The name of the game in dealing with dementia is adaptation since the condition is progressive. We must always adapt to the changes that come. If keeping the condition "under wraps" is beginning to limit your engagement in life, consider selectively revealing your diagnosis to others. Help people to know how to be with you. For example, ask that they speak clearly and slowly, refrain from side conversations that don't include you, and keep sentences short, clear and direct. And as you ask others to accommodate some of your needs, you will be adapting to your needs as well, helping yourself with new strategies. If you enjoy parties but notice that large gatherings have become too loud or overwhelming, consider calling ahead and asking for a quiet area to take needed breaks. Rest before the party, and plan to rest after. If you don't enjoy the larger gathering at all, call those that you looked forward to seeing at the party to come for a one-on-one visit in the week or two after the party, find out how the party was and enjoy a more intimate conversation. If you need a ride to accommodate your driving limitations, ask the driver if he or she would be willing to leave if you become overwhelmed or fatigued.

What Can be Done? Advocacy

In the study by O'Connor and colleagues mentioned earlier, many participants noted that they could use their knowledge and their personal experiences to educate others, and to "move the needle" on resisting stigmas surrounding dementia. At the same time, they used peer support opportunities to "lead" others newly diagnosed, helping them to take charge of their diagnosis and providing language for educating others. Many people living with dementia find purpose and meaning in advocacy.

The Scotland Early Onset Alzheimer's Disease Group Story

I visited Scotland with colleagues and was given the opportunity to visit with several individuals living with dementia who were associated with Alzheimer Scotland.[44] At one social center, we met a wonderful group of individuals and had tea. They described the power of coming together to support each other with stories of strength and hope, coping strategies, and friendship without stigma. They had designed and wear bracelets that say "Alzheimer's". Walter, a soft-spoken, clear-eyed, dapper gentleman leaned in toward me and asked, "Do you know why we've done this? Several reasons. To increase awareness. People ask me about my bracelet and then I can educate them. On a bad day, I can summon help, just by pointing to my wrist. And lastly, you know the AIDS rights groups? Like them, we are proud to be seen. We are not going to be shamed by our diagnosis."

The Quiet Advocate

And if you don't want to become a public advocate? There is much to be done in your own circle of family and friends. Ask that people use empowering language. Ask that people are direct. If you are like many PLWD, you may not ask directly – is there someone who you can confide in and make your wishes known to others? Can you post or pass along a declaration of rights on language as posted on Kate Swaffer's website:

---
44   www.alzscot.org

https://kateswaffer.com/2014/10/07/the-power-of-language/? Go to review her list and pick those that are important to you. Make a small card to pass to those important to you to begin to educate and hopefully change the behavior of your circle of friends and family. Be forgiving as individuals begin their change. They are changing a lifetime of bias, but you can help them move to a more dementia-friendly place.

These actions will begin to move conversations forward to open, honest dialogues. It will help those who will be your advocates know your wishes for when they may need to assist in your decision-making. The purpose of this book is to accompany you on the journey in the way that you wish – living for today, and molding the behaviors of those around you, will improve your day-to-day. They/we don't mean to be disrespectful, but this is an area that has not been met with a human rights approach – it has been kept in the shadows. You will do a great service to bring it to the light.

The Consummate Teacher

Dr. Walsh's Story

Dr. Walsh was neat in his tweed jacket and bow tie. Soft-spoken, gracious, and held in his gaze, one always felt center stage when engaged by him. He truly knew how to listen. He was a clinician and teacher – but I believe he led with teaching, whether it was his patients, his students, his trainees, or his colleagues. He was a champion for geriatric care. He always taught by example. He noticed that he was having trouble with word finding and a few other symptoms and came to me for an evaluation and diagnosis: mixed dementia – probable Alzheimer's disease with vascular component. He sat, nodding and holding his wife's hand, as we reviewed the information. After a few minutes of silence, he said quietly, "I think I will tell everyone and tell them what I need." His voice grew in volume. "It will help them all know how to interact with me and maybe others." It took Dr. Walsh only a few minutes to put the diagnosis into perspective and find a way forward. I suspect he had been giving it thought for months before this appointment. He looked me in the eye and said, "I may lose a few friends, but I will build a team." He had helped so many with the diagnosis in the past, and he was now preparing to help himself and his family.

How do you build this team that Dr. Walsh speaks of? Kate Swaffer, the advocate for persons living with dementia you met earlier in the chapter, provides recommendations.[45]

Learning about communication strategies may be helpful. Ask your physician for a referral to an occupational therapist or a speech therapist who are specialty trained to work with those with dementia. Ask the therapist for suggestions on communication techniques for you and for communicating with others. Ask whether your selected family member may accompany you to your sessions, to take notes and review the suggestions with you once your sessions with the therapist are over. For group trainings, look for specialists in your area or on-line. In Connecticut, LiveWell,[46] a nonprofit focused exclusively on caring for individuals at all stages of Alzheimer's disease and related dementia, hosts several programs to foster communication and independence – some educational components may be on-line.

---

45 https://kateswaffer.com/2014/06/05/20-things-not-to-say-or-do-to-a-person-with-dementia/
46 https://livewell.org/

The Memory Bridge,[47] founded by Michael Verde in 2003, is a community of people focusing on communication guided by those living with dementia. The organization provides trainings in challenging beliefs and enhancing communication around dementia. The group has used their connections and creativity to partner and spread the message with schools and hospices. Check out Memory Bridge news section on their website to see how they've created these connections. Do these connections in other communities inspire you to create something similar in your own community?

Why We Need to Resist Stigma?

Why do so many of us remain quiet or silent? "To face social scrutiny and ridicule is the price we pay for transparency, and why become a martyr when you can effectively pass as someone without HIV? There is safety in assimilation. There is safety in invisibility," reports Arik Hartmann when speaking about living with HIV.[48] I understand this. I think anyone does. To have a condition that is not well-received by the public makes us want to remain undetected. But since we feel the need to hide, the chance that we become isolated increases. When isolated and not connected, our chance for addiction to whatever soothes us will increase. According to Johann Hari, if we are isolated, we will go into despair. We will bond with something to relieve our pain, like food, pornography, cannabis, or alcohol, for example. When we allow stigma to keep us isolated, we will fall into despair. Possibly we can extrapolate studies on

---

47 https://www.memorybridge.org/
48 https://www.ted.com/talks/arik_hartmann_our_treatment_of_hiv_has_advanced_why_hasn_t_the_stigma_changed/up-next#t-310190

addiction and isolation to dementia and isolation. Portugal has decriminalized drugs and spent the money on reconnecting the previous addicts into society, assisting them in finding purpose and meaning. This approach cut drug addiction by 50 percent.[49] The take-home point is this: get a purpose. Find a purpose you believe in and begin to volunteer. Give when and how you can. If you need to adapt a schedule, communication, transportation – please do! It will be worth it. Find or create a peer-support group. The work in the group will help you find purpose, if only in working as a volunteer. Your experience will help others. It works in 12-step programs; it works with individuals living with dementia. The Dementia Peer Coalition, a U.S.-based peer-to-peer support group, co-founded by Bob Savage (a person living with dementia) and Stephani Shivers, OT, M.Ed., meets via Zoom (an internet-based meeting platform) to offer support and encouragement to each other.[50]

Arik Hartmann discusses facing ridicule and social scrutiny as a result of his efforts to increase transparency and ultimately fight ignorance. He says it is important to spread education to this ignorance, since "ignorance is not synonymous with stupid. It's not the inability to learn. It's the state you're in before you learn." The individuals in the Alzheimer Scotland group used their Alzheimer's bracelets to increase awareness. Others may work to change policy. The reality is that once people know someone with a condition, they are likely to build their capacity to see the humanity in the individual and expand that humanity to the condition, whatever that stigmatized condition or

---

[49] Hari Johann TED talk https://www.ted.com/talks/johann_hari_everything_you_think_you_know_about_addiction_is_wrong/up-next
[50] https://dementiapeercoalition.wordpress.com/about-2/

experience may be, whether it's Alzheimer's disease, mental illness, drug addiction, or being gay, just to name a few.

Points to Remember

- Stigma is a real part of the diagnosis of dementia – the culture, including family, friends and even in ourselves.
- Most of the information on dementia is given voice by those who do not have dementia. Kate Swaffer reminds us that until we hear from people living with dementia, the stigma won't change.[51]
- Many people living with dementia hold the same stigma regarding dementia as do others, and that stigma may stop them from participating.
- Isolation worsens quality of life and often leads to depression.
- Disclosing the diagnosis of dementia to others is a personal choice. Understand the implication of disclosure or limiting disclosure to make an informed choice.

Action Plan

- Begin the process of reconceptualizing your life from independent or dependent to the reality that we are all interdependent. Keep a diary of when you need help, but as importantly, when you are able to be helpful. Grow your understanding that life is full of give and take.
- Consider how you can be an advocate for de-stigmatizing dementia, whether quietly, in your own circle of friends and

---

51   https://kateswaffer.com/2014/10/07/the-power-of-language/

family, or more broadly. There are several suggestions in this chapter to move forward. Journal on what would help you move forward on one of them. Commit to that.

- Understand that isolation will perpetuate the stigma and decrease your sense of well-being. Push through any discomfort and think of "connecting" as a therapeutic necessity, much more powerful than any medication. Commit to one "connecting" activity.

Resources

Kate Swaffer, *What the Hell Happened to My Brain?*

Author, advocate, and activist, Ms. Swaffer has compiled poems, blog posts, and chapters on the experience living with early onset Alzheimer's disease. She received an advanced degree in Gerontology focusing on stigma. She is well-versed in this area, from both an academic and a personal perspective. Her passion for improving the life of those living with dementia is evident on every page.

Mary Pipher, *Woman Rowing North*

A cultural anthropologist and psychologist, Mary Pipher uses her clinical experience in addressing attitudes that inhibit growth with aging and challenges the way we think about ourselves. Pipher meant for the book to be a guidebook for enhancing what is possible, challenging the cultural thoughts that limit us. Her book focuses on women and ageism, but the tenets can be extrapolated to the stigma that surrounds dementia.

Chapter 4

COMMUNICATION AND COMMUNICATION CHANGES

The Kenny Family Story

I was visiting my mother several times a year during her early years of dementia. We lived 1500 miles apart and I would fly out to visit about every six weeks. I was a busy working mother and time seemed so limited, rushed, urgent. I would sit down with my mother for a cup of tea to catch up. My mom would start to tell a story but falter in her words, and I would jump in ... guessing, pantomiming, finishing her sentences. Patience is not one of my virtues. My mom would at first do nothing, but as the conversation and my interruptions continued, she would flash me a look, her lips would thin into a tight grimace, and she would go silent. I would be jolted back to the present. I had told patients and their families to be patient, slow conversation down, wait for responses, watch non-verbal responses, ask before offering word-finding suggestions. I knew better but I didn't stop myself. I reached across the bistro table and placed my hand on my mom's arm. "I'm sorry. I'm rushing." She looked up, still angry. I took a few deep breaths. *"I really am sorry – I don't have the kids or work with me. I will slow down. I promise!"* She looked at me warily. Could she trust me? Who knows? I had to make this apology many, many times. But in time, my mother's honesty with her angry eyes and silence did train me.

Communication Changes Due to Dementia

There is so much to communication. Communication is how we maintain our relationships, so when cognitive changes diminish our ability to speak and communicate, it may strain our relationships and affect our self-esteem. It is worth finding workarounds that build on the strengths you have and acknowledge any weaknesses caused by the neural loss.

What is aphasia? Aphasia is the term used to describe losing the ability to speak and to understand speech. Aphasia includes both processing the language to communicate and understanding what is said.

Dementia takes years to advance over stages, the symptoms worsening in each subsequent stage. In the early stages, someone can carry on normal conversations but will simply forget a word or use the wrong words (anomia). Resuming a conversation after an interruption may become difficult. These communication hiccups happen all the time to most people, but dementia affects the brain so that language problems become more noticeable. Someone with Alzheimer's, for instance, won't remember phrases, or struggle learning new phrases. Slang and common expressions become difficult or even impossible to remember. Someone with dementia may start confusing the meaning of words, saying "I want worms for dinner" instead of asking for their favorite spaghetti, or calling a computer "the picture." It is also more challenging for people with dementia to hold multiple ideas in their thoughts at once, so they may jump from topic to topic without completing a coherent conversation or becoming frustrated as they struggle to complete one topic without losing track of the second.

Additionally, understanding may be affected. Agnosia is the inability to understand sensations, and this may include the written or spoken word, depending on what part of the brain is affected by dementia or a stroke. More generally, the words heard by a brain affected by Alzheimer's disease may be compromised by other factors. If someone speaks quickly, in a high-pitched voice, with an accent foreign to the person living with dementia, or using complex speech, a person living with dementia may struggle to follow the conversation. Many of my patients tell me they just agree with whatever is being said, rather than asking for clarity, as it happens often.

Strategies that May Help with Communication

I'd like to give tips that come from the mouths of my patients or from the writings of those living with dementia. Make these known to friends and family to begin to assist them in knowing how to communicate with you. Add whatever seems most meaningful to you to the list.

Here are some of the strategies we use at the institution that I work at, honed from several discussions with persons living with dementia.

- Slow the pace of discussion and allow time for PLWD to process and respond.

- Simplify sentences or choices.
- Ask one question at a time.
- Speak clearly and calmly, be patient and understanding, and listen.
- Avoid arguing with or embarrassing the PLWD.
- Treat the PLWD with dignity and respect.
- Meet in a quiet place without extra noise or distractions (such as side conversations).
- Be aware of body language; make eye contact and connect.

Some verbal strategies include asking for short and simple sentences, ask the listener to repeat back what they heard for confirmation that you were heard correctly, asking for paraphrasing – again for confirmation that the words were heard correctly – and staying with one idea or concept at a time. You could have a card ready to communicate these strategies to your guest or family member. Begin the card with a reminder that this is to help communication and as a reminder until everyone is practiced in these new strategies.

Environmental modifications can also help your communication. Eye contact and physical touch remind both parties to remain present. Eliminate or avoid background distractions, such as a television or party. Finding a side room at a large family gathering to hold a one-on-one conversation, as a break from the bigger party, and to make a personal connection, can enhance the communication with a special someone.

The Role of Speech Therapy in Cognitive Loss

Speech therapy is a great way for people to maintain a level of independence for longer. It helps stimulate cognitive ability through activities associated with the underlying cognitive changes.

The speech therapist or pathologist teaches strategies to compensate for communication deficits. The speech therapist may suggest ways to modify the environment or offer strategies to adapt to the ongoing cognitive changes caused by dementia. For example, they can work on memory retrieval strategies, such as spaced retrieval, errorless learning, or the use of cognitive aids, such as memory books and other types of external memory aids (e.g., using notebooks, notes on your phone, timers on your watch).

Expression Beyond Verbal Communication

It is important to remember to use all forms of communication. Much of our communication is not verbal. Could it be in a written story? In a piece of art? A type of dance?

Jacqueline Woodson, an author and TED talk speaker, talks about reading slowly.[52] In it, she talks about her ancestors who were not allowed to read or write, but were able to communicate through song, quilting, sitting on the stoop and talking, to keep the story alive. What can we do? Is there a grandchild who can help us with documenting our story when we sit on the stoop? Can our daughter "play" in an art form that helps us express ourselves? Does poetry, with the freedom from syntax

---

[52] https://www.ted.com/talks/jacqueline_woodson_what_reading_slowly_taught_me_about_writing/details

and sentence structure, allow enough words to get our meaning from us. Does dance?

Tony and Doris' Story

Doris was a woman of few words when I met her, but she spoke volumes with her smile and doleful eyes that sometimes would flash a bright sparkle. Tony would start our sessions, tense and easily frustrated, trying to convey issues that he felt weren't going well at home. "Dr. Kenny, sometimes she just won't eat!" he would say, his voice rising. Doris would touch his arm and put her hand out, palm up. "Doris, one minute, I need to have Dr. Kenny understand." Doris would smile meekly, touch him again, and hold her hand out, palm up. Tony would look at her and visibly melt. He would look at me, smile, stand, and ask her to dance, placing his hand in her outstretched hand. Doris would hold him and dance him into calmness. "Dr. Kenny, she does this all the time. She asks me to dance when I start stressing out that I'm not good enough to help her. And, when she holds me, I know that dancing with her is all she really needs – the rest will wait." Doris smiles at me, a knowing woman-to-woman exchange that implies we must take care of this poor, lost soul until he understands that it is all that ever mattered. All that said with a hand and a smile.

There are programs that have been developed to enhance engagement through the arts, rather than based on only language or memory. A well-established and researched program found to be helpful is TimeSlips.[53] The training is relatively

---

53 timeslips.org

inexpensive and provides training and a warehouse of 300 creativity prompts grounded in a training based in the core values of humanity, joy and creativity.

Augmentation to Verbal Communication

There are several communication methods that may augment or circumvent the difficulty with language. Taking the time early in the disease to prepare for the changes that will likely come or are beginning can be very helpful.

Kelly and June

I was introduced to Kelly and June by a close friend. Kelly had been recently diagnosed with mild cognitive impairment (MCI) and wanted to talk about issues that may come up in the future in a relaxed setting, not in a doctor's office. We sat in a light-filled, beautiful living space, sipping on sparkling wine. Kelly was happy and curious while June sat nearby, supportive and encouraging. Kelly described how she was doing very well, walking and eating correctly, staying engaged in community, but that the COVID pandemic was limiting her ability to socialize. We were discussing how staying engaged would continue to help limit the loss of language – the "use it or lose it" concept. Kelly said she believes that her symptoms are not progressing, that all communication remains completely intact, that she has not noticed a change in her ability to communicate, that likely she won't have language issues with her cognitive loss. June's eyebrows raised slightly, and she laid her hand on Kelly's arm. "I notice that you ask questions over and over and that you don't always understand conversations when we have a few people over." Kelly looked at me quizzically. "Individuals often don't realize the impact of the disease on their function," I said. "Unfortunately, it is part of the disease process not to recognize the deficits. This aspect of the disease can keep people from seeking help." Kelly looked at me and said, "Well, I guess I was hoping this wouldn't hit me or might just go away, but this is no time for denial! Let's get to work, what do I do to prepare?"

Kelly's willingness to prepare is perfect. The energy she puts into preparing for loss in communication will be very helpful. She can create strategies now that will help her in her future.

Consider building "communication supplements" now that may help later. Some ideas include a *picture board*, which is a board for words you need to use frequently. If you are beginning to slip in knowing something you need often, make a sign for it. Begin a *personal communication dictionary*. A personal communication dictionary contains information about unique communication behaviors. It provides information about what a person does, then what it means, and suggests options for what the other person should do in response. These are often written for those who are not as familiar with the individual who needs augmentation to their communication. It can be used for those who may participate in your care to help them understand when a behavior may signal a clue to your feelings, wants, or needs. A personal information dictionary usually is set up in three columns. The behavior or action is in the first column, the possible meaning is in the second column, and the suggested approach is in the third column. I have noticed, for example, certain behaviors or actions of mine that signify distress. If I begin to scratch my head or notice that my scalp or legs feel itchy, it often signifies I'm tired or overwhelmed and in need of a rest. Of course, it could mean that I have a bug bite or dry skin, and these can easily be ruled out, but nine times out of 10, I'm tired. If I bite my thumb nail, I'm worried or anxious, and someone may want to soothe me in some way such as with a smile, a hand on my shoulder, or a brief walk. These are examples of what I might write to begin my own personal information dictionary. You do not have to make the chart, but if you investigate your actions or begin to ask those you live with for examples on what they've noticed about you, you can begin to document these clues in some way. Keep a running list in this journal, and it may become helpful in the future.

Gina's Story

Gina walked across the waiting area beaming. Her smile, her step, her cadence were ebullient. Seeing her lifted my spirits, and I asked with curiosity, "What's new? even though I was thinking, "What's happened to you?" Gina said that on our last visit, she had taken to heart the request to be curious. The request to be curious stemmed from noticing what soothes her and what invigorates her. The request had come after she had reported some irritability and lack of motivation. "Dr. Kenny, you mentioned I should look at everything, but especially things that bypass just thinking, such as art, nature, and music. It's been my fun little mission. I've tried all kinds of music stations on Pandora, and I take notes on how they make me feel! When I felt sluggish, I tried walking, yoga, looking at art books, and upbeat music. It's the music that works for me! It perks me up enough that I can drag myself out for a walk. Once I walked on a tree-lined path near my house. That really helped me feel a pick me up, but walking in my neighborhood did not – that makes me edgy. It has been so interesting. I'm learning so much about myself and learning to listen to the signals of my body."

Gina's story illustrates how our bodies speak to us. The brain may be changing, but we can adapt. Greg O'Brien writes in On Pluto that he knows to remove himself from a situation when he feels rage emerging. He also mentions that a beer and a discussion looking out at the water soothes him. I'm learning from people living with dementia to look for these experiences as well. I'm learning to camp, to keep my brain stimulated, and to immerse myself in nature. I write this as I sit at a campsite overlooking a beautiful lake with a cool breeze rustling the branches and making me pause to appreciate this moment of calm.

Expand your Communication Using the Arts

How can we explore a creative side? Greg O'Brien in On Pluto mentions several of his personal heroes living with dementia who embraced their creativity and found meaning in new ways to communicate. The Reverend Cynthia Huling Hummel is an example. She wrote *UnMasking Alzheimer's: The Memories Behind the Masks*. She took a class on mask-making and used masks to communicate some of her feelings, strengths, and sorrows regarding dementia. There are several classes supported through art museums, often based on the Museum of Modern Art's Alzheimer's Project that resulted in the 2009 guide *Meet Me: Making Art Accessible to People with Dementia*,[54] or the Rockville, MD-based Arts for Aging offers virtual workshops

---

54 https://www.moma.org/visit/accessibility/meetme/

and programing.[55] As mentioned above, Timeslips is a program that features storytelling. Look for art programs supported in your area.

What if you do not have access to a class or a program that interests you? Julia Cameron's *The Artist's Way* is a workshop in a book. Each chapter explores an activity or potential barrier to opening to your creative self. The book can be approached chapter by chapter, taking a week at a time or even a month per chapter. It could be done in a group setting or by yourself. It can also be used a la carte – selecting activities or choices throughout the book without going in a sequential way. It recommends weekly artist dates that have you explore something of interest or new to you. This can be done outside your home or with activities within your house or via the internet. Use it as an idea generator. Let it help you get out of your thinking brain and into your creative self. We are looking for ways to open ourselves up and communicate. We are looking for ways to express.

Some people dictate or write a series of stories from their lives to aid in communication and engagement to be used when their disease begins to take their language. This allows for meaningful springboards for connection. A gentleman I worked with had been involved in theater and motion pictures. He was proud of that connection. He compiled pictures and playbills and wrote brief stories and anecdotes about his experiences.

---

55   https://artsfortheaging.org/programs

Communication Around End-of-Life Wishes

Emotional Blocks to Communication, Especially Around End-of-Life Choices

We know that when someone doesn't feel heard, they often shut down and begin to not speak, whether this is due to stigma – others' or our own – or the changes in our brains due to dementia. The culture around dementia and dementia itself may render us mute. But, if we stop talking due to the stigma or the hurt from not being heard, we will hasten the problem further. Can going to a speech therapist help? Is there someone in your family or friends circle who is willing to do "speech" exercises with you? It should be someone you trust and are willing to practice talking with – play acting will even help. Could you select talking topics from a book of prompts for creative writing, or telling your opinion about a short piece read to you by another? Be creative in keeping your voice practiced.

Add to this the difficulty in speaking about what you'd like for your end-of-life story. Can you take some of the communication skills and begin some of the hard conversations? How to begin? Speak about how you want to live! Fill in the story with what makes your day-to-day happy and meaningful. Talk about what brings you joy. And then from there, it will aid you in seeing and articulating what you may not want. I can imagine enjoying watching my children and my grandchild interacting, even if I do so with quiet eyes. But, if my days were filled with fear, if my heart was racing with each person that came through the door or into the institution, and my family could not find a way to calm me, I do not think that would be a quality that I would want. I would give my children the latitude to offer me medications and markedly limit medical interventions to extend my life. I would want them to begin the process of letting go of me in this world. I have had these conversations. And I will expand them as more ideas come to me. I know we cannot plan for all the ups and downs of life, but we can help our families by letting them know our thoughts about how we would want to be in that life.

What if the Emotional Block Comes From Those Speaking to You?

People living with dementia are often excluded from conversations because of a perception that they are incapable of participating due to cognitive decline. Bob Savage, co-founder of the Connecticut-based Dementia Peer Coalition, calls it "dementiatized." You can (and I suggest, must) stop people and make sure they know your desire to remain in meaningful communication.

There are few studies to help us know what constitutes meaningful communication for people living with dementia. You know what you think for yourself, but I offer what the meager literature reveals to give you language to use with those you live with or engage with to assist them in aiding in continuing in communication with you. In one of the rare studies that asked individuals living with dementia what they valued, Sarah Alsawy and colleagues recorded interactions between several individuals living with dementia and their care partners. The researchers then asked the person living with dementia their impressions of the conversations. The PLWD offered thoughts that went beyond suggestions to minimize distractions or ask simple questions. They reported that the intention of wanting to communicate was often as important to them as actually understanding what was being said; the emotional connection was paramount. They also reported that valuing the intention of the other party to empower their communication, whether by paying attention to their non-verbals or by making physical contact that encouraged continuation of the effort to communicate, was important. Finally, the PLWD reported that communication was inhibited when they were made to feel inferior, or someone did not hear them (as indicated by being "talked over").[56]

Knowing this may help you guide your family in how best to communicate with you as you progress through the disease. Remind them:

- Lead with their heart! Make the intention of what they want to communicate be the most important aspect of the communication – love, safety, caring.
- Ask them to work to empower your communication – have them look for those non-verbals, such as your mood.
- Ask them to always strive to make you feel like an equal partner – remember your humanness. No talking down or patronizing.

Sam and Lavonne's story

Sam, a steely-eyed gentleman with gray peppered throughout his hair, sat across from me and his daughter, Lavonne. "Doctor Anne, tell Lavonne what you told me ... that this dementia-thing I have will one day get so bad that I won't want to live with it

---

[56] Alsawy S, Mansell W, McEvoy P, Tai S. What is good communication for people living with dementia? A mixed-methods systematic review. Int Psychogeriatr. 2017 Nov;29(11):1785-1800. doi: 10.1017/S1041610217001429. Epub 2017 Jul 31. PMID: 28756788.

anymore." Lavonne, thin and stern, looked shocked at her father and then turned an angry eye at me. "You did not tell him that! How could you?" "Now Lavonne, leave the nice doctor alone. She told me I would live a long time with this causing little troubles that we would manage the best we can. But one day, I will lose more than my memory – I won't walk right or eat right. I don't want that. She said I need to let my people know what I want if I want to avoid getting too much care at the end and prolonging my time in the bad stage. And I don't want to use all my money up, caring for my body when I could use it on you kids." Lavonne had been looking down as her father spoke, not making eye contact, holding her hands tightly clasped in her lap. "No," Lavonne looked up sharply and shot back when she heard the last comment. "Dad, we will spend whatever we need to. We will make sure you get the best care!" "Lavonne, you aren't listening to me!" Sam said sadly. "No, I will not discuss this. Not with you or with her," said Lavonne. "We are not talking about you dying – you are fine, and you will be fine. I will see to that!" Lavonne stood rapidly and walked out the door saying, "I will meet you in the lobby when you are done!"

Communicating what you'd like your end-of-life choices to be is often a difficult topic to initiate and one that many will not want to hear. Greg O'Brien in *On Pluto* describes his father's reluctance to discuss end-of-life wishes with him or his mother.

"In the final months, our dinner table discussions centered around topics we had never entertained before. End-of-life stuff. My father ... probed knotty questions about what happens to you when you die. A rock-ribbed Catholic who had lost both his parents in childhood, he feared death, and like many of us, wasn't quite sure of what awaited him on the other side. He was deathly afraid. Mom seemed to embrace it." After his father had died, Greg sat with his wife discussing whether his mother should be moved from her family home to a nursing home closer to his siblings. Greg had not thought his mother could hear him or understand him, in her grief and cognitive loss.

"Greg," my mother interrupted, breaking fifteen minutes of staring silence. 'GREG,' she shouted. 'THAT'S NOT A GOOD IDEA. IT'S JUST NOT A GOOD IDEA!' She looked staring at me like a mother disciplining a son."

She finally made her wishes known to her son.[57]

My mother did the same when we (her children) knew she could no longer live in a house alone. At the final hour, my mother, like Greg O'Brien's mother, pulled all her energy together, to let us know our choice was not her choice and that if she must move, she was going to move to a place she thought was best. And she did. It's best if all these choices are made in advance -- not everyone I've met has had their children listen to them in the final hour.

Greg O'Brien tells several stories of facing death – his own, his friends, his mentors – in a chapter of On Pluto titled "Out to the Jupiter Belt." On a day when he was dealing with both prostate cancer and the diagnosis of Alzheimer's disease, he "resolves to take my life." But in seeing the beauty of Narragansett Bay, "I resolved to focus on my wife, kids, and work, and whatever else happens, it just happens. ... I can't control the rest, I reasoned, nor could my mom. Gotta learn to walk in faith." The chapter is filled with beautiful vignettes of how others dealt

---

[57] Greg O'Brien, On Pluto: Inside the Mind of Alzheimer's (2014)

with facing the end of their lives: his primary care doctor, Pat, a friend named Hilly, his friend and mentor Malcolm. Greg finishes the chapter by contemplating the obituary that will be written when he is dead, once that day comes, "But today is not that day. Inside the mind of Alzheimer's isn't such a bad place to be on this cloudy fall day. There's clarity to it, as I await the sunrise of the new morning, secure that the sun will set at dusk, hoping to see it rise yet again, knowing that one day it will not, as I drift further out into the Milky Way looking for my mother."

Sam, from our story above, had two wishes that he wanted to articulate. The first was his desire to avoid the latest stages of the disease by limiting medical interventions at a certain point in his illness, much as Greg O'Brien discussed in the quote above. His second wish (and a concern) was using excessive resources for care at the late stage of disease. Many feel this way, but families are reluctant to adjust treatment for fear this will be seen as neglect or selfishness. If it is your wish, be sure to frame the request as part of the financial legacy you would like to leave, along with your wishes for passing on words of wisdom or memories of meaningful exchanges.

What can be done if a family member does not want to listen or discuss? Most will come around if given some time and patience. Putting your wishes into writing or a video can allow the family member to read/watch in their own time and space, have a reaction, and come to a place where they may be able to talk or pose questions. They may need to pose questions via written response first. Allow them this container for their reactions before requesting they discuss the topic with you in person.

Points to Remember

- Communication changes often accompany dementia – both the ability to understand what is being said and the ability to generate language. Begin to be aware of the changes so that you can adapt or institute workarounds.
- Many people will withdraw from conversations when those conversations become difficult – please fight this urge and assist others in communicating more effectively with you.
- Speech therapy can be helpful in personal assessment of your communication needs and developing personalized strategies that can help with maintaining communication.
- Verbal communication is only one type of communication. Do you have another way that you like to express yourself, such as song, written word, art or dance?
- There are strategies that can augment communication, such as picture boards and personal communication dictionaries.
- Look to the arts for an expansion of your communication and expression.
- Have the courage to stay in the conversations – even when your communication may be changing. And especially, have the courage to speak about how you'd like to live your life and what would be your limit for when you want that living to shift to accepting your death.

Action Items

- Make a card with strategies that will help you in communication. Carry it with you and hand it to those communicating with you to assist them in knowing how to slow the

conversation, make points clearly, find a quiet environment, etc.
- Consult with a speech therapist (preferably one that understands dementia and strategies for communication in dementia).
- Begin to put together a list of personal communication hints – what calms you, agitates you, or gets your creative juices flowing. These hints can help in your future when others may have to call on these hints for enhancing your quality of life.
- Schedule time to reflect and then hold conversations to discuss how you want to live and when you feel living would shift to dying with those that need to hear these conversations. If they cannot "hear" you, leave some type of message – written, dictated, video – whatever you feel will get your message across.

Resources

Greg O'Brien, On Pluto: Inside the Mind of Alzheimer's

Greg O'Brien is a writer, editor, investigative reporter, and publisher who was diagnosed with early onset Alzheimer's disease. In *On Pluto*, he uses his excellent writing skills to describe what it is like to experience dementia embedded in the story of his life in a large Irish, Catholic family. He also speaks with the voice of a caregiver, as both his mother and father lose their lives to dementia. His insights and metaphors and his fighting spirit give the reader an interesting example of the good, the bad and the ugly of showing up every day facing life, and ultimately grappling with the thought of death, with Alzheimer's dementia.

Julia Cameron, The Artist's Way

The Artist's Way is the seminal book on the subject of creativity. It is a creativity workshop in a book. It has been read by millions of people and helped them find ways through blocks to creativity. It is a workbook and is full of creativity exercises. It can be used just explore and pique your interest in trying new projects and explore your past passions or obstacles. Many of the exercises include journaling about your past and what has made you tick, so the exploration will be excellent for preparing to live your life to the fullest presently and may assist in making plans for the future as well.

Chapter 5

LEGACY

The Kenny Family Story

My mother's legacy was a lived one. She left her children with values and life examples. We laugh easily and hold a sense of play and wonder because our mother did. We all played on the floor, in the snow, curled up on the couch because our mother did. We each worked to make her laugh; the laugh that left her doubled over, gasping for breath, unable to speak, and tears rolling down her face. During the time of pandemic, my siblings and I meet for a weekly telephone/video get togethers. These video meetings continue as travel restrictions were lifted and we also travel to meet in person. We discuss books, movies, television shows, our lives, and our families. But most cherished, we tell stories of our memories of our mother and father, our grandparents, our deceased brothers. We do so to fill in the gaps for each other, to broaden and enhance the stories, to learn our family stories and lessons from another perspective, and to keep our family story alive. It is such a gift – this intergenerational passing of our family story. The stories have moved me to tears. The stories open my heart. But often, and best of all, I've joined my siblings doubled over, unable to speak, laughing so hard I can't catch my breath. Best legacy of all – the genetic ability to laugh fully.

Overview

Contemplating legacy helps us frame our lives. Dr. Elizabeth Hunter, an occupational therapist and investigator from the University of Kentucky, writes "Legacies proved to be strongly individual yet still share a common human element, that of making meaning of life. More than merely leaving behind a mark of some kind, or giving away one's possessions, legacy creation provided a means to fulfill the deeper need of creating a coherent end to the twists and turns of fate that typified each woman's life story."[58]

I find this definition amazing: "creating a coherent end to the twist and turns." We all have these twists and turns, and they are what make our lives unique. Let's take the time, in this chapter, to review in what way we may create a coherent story we would like to leave behind, to describe how these twists and turns have shaped us. It may be something tangible, a body of work, or a personal story. All are wonderful – each is personal. Now is the time to contemplate and plan for what that legacy should be.

---

[58] Hunter, Elizabeth G. Beyond Death: inheriting the past and giving to the Future, transmitting the legacy of oneself, Omega volume 56; 313-329, 2007/2008

Legacy of Self

Generativity

The renowned human developmental expert Erik Erikson, Ph.D., posits that the final stages of psychosocial development focus on generativity (vs. stagnation) and ego integrity (vs. despair). Generativity is the sense of "making your mark" on the world, addressing the questions of what are my accomplishments and what have I done to make the world a better place? We often focus on making commitments to other people (family, children, life partner), contributing to the next generation and mentoring others. The more individuals have developed positive relationships, and have been involved in their community, the more likely they are to feel greater fulfillment. Major life changes, as may happen at the time of the diagnosis with dementia, often trigger a search for meaning. This is a time that may spark a need to strengthen relationships (including making amends) or increase community involvement.

Christine Bryden, a woman living with Alzheimer's dementia, did just that. She strengthened and evolved her relationship with her daughters, established a new, intimate, and courageous relationship with Paul and went on to marry him, began and completed an advanced degree in theology, wrote three books, and became an advocate for persons living with dementia. She describes much of this in her book, *Before I Forget*.

She says, "It was not until I had been able to overcome my sense of hopelessness that I was able to begin to overcome my actual helplessness. So, with my newfound motivation from my talks with Liz (her spiritual counselor), I remember announcing to my specialist in 1996 that I was planning to write a book.

He said he'd look forward to reading it. Then I nervously asked him how long I'd have to write it. How long before I couldn't write anymore? Couldn't remember to write anymore? 'I can't tell you that,' he said. 'Everyone's different. But if I were you, I'd get started as soon as possible."[59]

How do we shake ourselves out of a sense of foreboding from this disease? Viktor Frankl, physician, and philosopher wrote *Man's Search for Meaning*, and countless people have used it as lessons for overcoming difficult situations. Frankl, by narrating his life in Auschwitz, a German concentration camp, presents the remarkable idea of how we can choose to see a purpose or meaning in any situation, including the worst conditions. Frankl developed a type of meaning-centered psychotherapy during his time as a prisoner in Auschwitz, from using his training and his observations of the reactions of those prisoners who survived and thrived, compared to those who did not. "Logotherapy focuses rather on the future, that is to say, on the meanings to be fulfilled by the patient in his future ... The patient is actually confronted with and reoriented toward the meaning of his life."[60]

A Guide to Building a Legacy of Self

The Legacy Project is the brainchild of Susan Bosak, who in a TEDx talk describes building a 7-Generation world. A 7-Generation world is a psychosocial way of being that fosters bigger thinking and action. Ms. Bosak suggests we orient our thoughts and actions grounded in the history of the three generations that

---

[59] Bryden, Christine. Before I Forget . Location 1645-1649 Penguin Books Ltd. Kindle version.
[60] Frankl, Viktor E.. Man's Search for Meaning (p. 98). Beacon Press. Kindle Edition.

come before us (our parents, grandparents, and great-grandparents) in the way we interact with family/neighbors and the world, and then build our legacy for how we will affect the three generations beyond us (our children, grandchildren and great-grandchildren). This concept brings together our past, present and future, and allows us to strategically connect to each other whether actual family or the community. Ms. Bosak recommends to "own it consciously and nurture it [our legacy] actively."

How would we do this? The Legacy Project website[61] poses questions to begin the adventure of a legacy of self-discovery in a format called Legacy Links. "It can be a meaningful exercise to celebrate the birth of a child or grandchild, or to honor the death of a parent or grandparent. A Legacy Link can be a blueprint for living and an intentional way to lay out your meaningful impact in the world."[62]

The idea of the Legacy Link is to create an "ethical will," passing on the meaning of your life in the context of three generations before you and to affect three generations into the future. While much of legacy is often facts and figures, the Legacy Project asks us to consider the "why" of our legacy – why does it matter that we pass something along?

Tony's Story

I partnered in care with Tony for as many years as I had been a doctor. He liked to wink at me as he told me he had trained me. He was right; he had trained me and still did. Tony had a tough life. I met him when he was managing his life very well.

---
61 www.legacyproject.org
62 https://legacyproject.org/7gen/legacylinks.html

Tony had a history of childhood abuse at the hands of his father and now he himself managed alcoholism. He told me he had become sober the day his wife left him, having finally heard one too many of his lies. She said he wouldn't see his daughter again if he didn't get help. So, he got help. He went to a rehabilitation facility and started an active life with the Twelve Steps of Alcoholics Anonymous. He did well, staying active in his daughter Tina's life. He spent weekends with Tina. He told me he saw her growing up, taught her to drive, witnessed her attend college ("First in our family to graduate!" he beamed), and watched her fall in love and marry. Tina now had a daughter of her own – Lisa. Tony noticed changes in his days. He forgot phone calls with his sponsor. He bounced a few checks and got into a fender bender. Tony asked if we could look into what was wrong. Tony's cognitive loss was consistent with Alzheimer's dementia. The diagnosis hit Tony hard, but he had a strong "family" in his recovery community and deep connection with his Higher Power to assist him. Tony gave up driving so that he wouldn't hurt himself or anyone else. He came to me with some deep sadness and said, "I have nothing to leave my daughter – no way to let her know how much she means to me. I have no money to pass on to her." I said, "Oh, Tony, no, but you've trained me and all your sponsees, and you have a thousand stories and life lessons from living in recovery." Tony replied, "I do help those who are struggling, but you know I can barely write." I asked if he could get his granddaughter, Lisa, who was in high school to help him. Tony lit up. He asked Lisa to visit him every Sunday morning. Tony made pancakes and told stories while Lisa typed them. When he was finished, Lisa helped him pick out pictures of Tina and herself that mattered most to Tony. They had them compiled and bound into a book. Tony told me he cried when Tina opened his gift – his legacy.

Christine Bryden also has a mission for her legacy work. She states, "In my writing, in my talks, and in my life, I don't dwell on the difficulties I face as a person with dementia because society has always focused on what people with dementia can't do; how 'difficult' we are, how disabled. My aim is to cut through all that, to remind the rest of the world that people with dementia are able to contribute, that we still need contact with the world. I've tried to emphasize the remaining abilities of people with dementia, and I haven't really gone into the dark and scary detail of living with dementia every day."[63]

What do you have to say? Who can help you capture those thoughts and words?

Tangible Legacy or Keepsakes

Kenny Family Story

My grandmother was a strong presence in my life. She lived with us for a few years in a large Midwestern city when I was about 9, but she missed the small town and moved home after a few years. My grandmother had a stroke when I was about 16 years old, and my mother and I went for an extended visit during her rehabilitation. It was during this visit that my grandmother shared stories with me that helped shape my opinions of death. My father had recently died, and the threat of losing my grandmother seemed overwhelming. Grandma sat and drank her tea.

---

63 Bryden, Christine. Before I Forget . position 2379-2382 Penguin Books Ltd. Kindle Edition

"Monkey (that was a pet name for me), during that stroke, I felt like I was hit by a train. No one wants that." She spoke with such directness. She asked me to bring picture frames or knick-knacks to her. She would tape a slip of paper to it with siblings' or cousins' names, and I would return the piece to her various collections. "What are you doing, Grandma?" I asked. "I'm selecting pieces I want to go to my family once I'm gone." So direct and matter-of-fact. "Grandma, you're not dying!" "Honey, we all die. I just want you all to have something to remember me. Something little but meaningful. I will be giving you these monkeys (old-fashioned wooden monkeys that held hands and could dangle from a shelf) because you've always been my little monkey." A few years later, when she did die, I received those monkeys and a scented heart that my grandfather had given her when they were courting, and some silver spoons. The heart and the silver spoons came with little notes – the piece of the gift I cherish the most. For the spoons, my grandmother said while the spoons will need to be polished, it will make the times that you will get together with your women friends all the more meaningful, and for the heart, my grandmother thought the scent was still there (though it was not … ahh, love!). It's the notes from my grandmother that are priceless to me.

Family left behind would love a legacy, a keepsake from their deceased family member – chosen by the individual – that represents a "story" from their lives together or a story that allows a window into the deceased's life. Letters, scrapbooks, photographs, audiotapes, videotapes, and other mementos can reinforce the happy recollection or explain the person. And it doesn't have to be happy – if the legacy story you would like to tell is one of strength or resilience, maybe the stories are full of the struggles you've overcome or the losses you've seen. What story do you want to live on in your family or friends?

Photographs/Photo Albums or Audio Recordings

Don't worry that it must be a big production. My brother and my sister are so very thoughtful. They take the time and trouble to make a curated small photo album of vacations, with a very few but thoughtful photos, memories, and "quotes" from the trip. These small books are just right. They are packed with memories and the highlights. The story of the trip comes flooding back with these few treasured triggers.

Think about audiotape (and transcription) to accompany any keepsake you put together, so that the recipient will know the "why" behind your choice – what makes this keepsake special to you? What emotion or story do you want to convey with the gift?

A dear friend cherishes a voicemail left by her father. He called and told her how much he enjoys Thanksgiving dinner, especially with her. He commented on the turkey and mashed potatoes with *lots* of gravy. So simple, but so meaningful to her. The lilt in his voice, the joy with which he emphasized the gravy. … That simple message spoke volumes to her of his love for her, his love of the ritual of family gathering, his playfulness, and how much he loved her gravy. She shines whenever she thinks of him and that simple, but loving, message.

Journals

Keep a journal for someone? A nightly or weekly few lines of information you would like them to know? For your spouse? Your children? Your grandchildren? What would you fill your journal with? The sky's the limit. Choose stories that mean something to you. My sister and I asked our mother for the story of how my father asked her to marry him, because each of us had "heard" a different version of the story. Why did you choose your career path? Who was most influential in your life and why?

The journal could be used for doodling if stories do not come, or for poetry if the syntax for a story has been lost due to dementia. The sky is truly the limit.

Jewelry/Furniture/Property/Land

If you are fortunate enough to leave someone something tangible such as jewelry, furniture, property, or land, consider leaving a record of any stories that accompany the piece. Was the jewelry a special gift? How does it hold meaning for you? Did you have your eye on that land for a special reason? Did you enjoy a favorite season on that land? Do you have family stories or annual rituals linked to the property? Be sure to pass the history along with the favored piece.

Books/Spiritual texts

Could your legacy be in the books you leave behind? Is there a collection that you curate for a certain child or grandchild that will change their life? Are there books that changed yours? Is it the lessons from those books or texts that you want to pass along?

My mother and I bonded over a few books as she was living with dementia but had lost some of her ability to communicate verbally. Together we read Mother Teresa of Calcutta's autobiography, No Greater Love. At points in our reading, my mother would squeeze my arm to stop my reading. It was her signal for me to read the last passage again and really soak in the meaning. She conveyed so much to me as we read that book together.

I know that many families have special spiritual texts that are passed along. Can you add the story of how that text impacted you in your life to add further meaning?

Hobbies (Sporting Goods/Tools/Hand crafts)

Was your love for a sport, a team, a craft, or a hobby what gave meaning to your life? Is there something from that enjoyment, that challenge, that creativity, that you would like your family members to understand? Can you plant a seed of the same passion in someone else? Is there a period in history you love and would love to pass some of that information and fascination on to a special grandchild?

This is just a time to consider. What makes your life tick? What has given you so much pleasure or pride that you'd like to share it with someone else? That is the stuff of legacy – spreading that piece of you through the next generations.

Community Legacy

Special Gifts and/or Endowments

Dr. W's Story

A mentor and colleague developed dementia. He had been a professor for many years. He was working well past the typical retirement age; seeing patients; teaching medical, nursing, pharmacy, and rehabilitation students and trainees in clinical settings; lecturing and writing about aging; and living well into advanced age. He had noticed that he was having some trouble with words, but thought that he might just be tired, as he had developed a malignancy, and had gone through surgery and a brief episode of chemotherapy to resolve the condition. He thought it had "taken it out of me, but I'm just not bouncing back like I'd like." He came to me to "see if there was anything else, anything that may make me struggle with words a bit?" He looked up at me sheepishly. He knew what could be causing him struggle with words, but he was reluctant to contemplate it. We had a discussion about testing his cognition and proceeded with the workup. He came in to discuss the results of his neurocognitive evaluation with me, accompanied by his loving wife. I confirmed that it appeared he was in the early stages of dementia. We held hands as I told him, and we both welled up with tears. We sat silently for a few minutes, while he processed what he had suspected but had hoped was not true. He then touched my cheek in a loving, fatherly way. "Anne, I'm going to make the best of this! I tell my patients to make the best of it, and I'm going to take my own advice." His wife smiled warmly at him. "I can make my mark in medicine in many ways, not just with teaching." Dr. W went on to endow a chair in geriatric medicine, specifically for an investigator working in dementia care. He contributed money to the medical school and had a commonly used multidisciplinary teaching room named in his honor, to recognize his multidisciplinary teaching philosophy. Dr. W set to work immediately leaving a legacy at his long-term place of employment to benefit leaders in his fields of passion

– geriatrics and education. He needed his wife's help to make this happen and to honor his intention for the endowment. He left a beautiful, personal tribute to his life's work.

Is there an organization or cause that you would like to support? A passion you would like to pass along? My children attended a high school that had an amazing legacy tradition. Each year, there was a special assembly for recipients of the several scholarships that were left by a family or an individual. Students were selected based on the values outlined in the scholarship brief, such as interests in nursing, disability, history, journalism, photography, etc. These gifts were not necessarily large, but they were important in that students were provided opportunities to be recognized for a strength other than academic success. Having these acknowledgements assist the student in differentiating themselves as they apply to college or work opportunities and provide a legacy for a value or passion as well as altruistic giving into the future.

Interested in a sustainable planet? Plant a tree. Value contemplative practice? Leave a bench to be used for rest and reflection. Desire world peace? Obtain permission to install or commission a peace pole at a school, place of worship, or neighborhood park. Speak to the administrator at your cherished organization to see what is possible or what is the best way to leave a legacy, considering your personal finances.

As noted above, Christine Bryden describes how when she was first diagnosed with dementia, she entered a period of helplessness and hopelessness. Then her perspective changed. She describes how in her lifetime she witnessed how her life work was helping others. "Noriko (a Japanese nurse who used Christine story to change how dementia is viewed in Japan) liked knowing that I had gone through doubt, denial, and fear on the way to acceptance of my dementia. She liked the idea of calling life after a diagnosis 'the beginning of a new journey.' She said, in a letter to me that year, 'My experiences tell me that suffering from dementia is not as horrible as what many people might think, because in some ways the disease shows a different, unknown way of living one's life and … can be a lofty challenge, even a growth process, in life.' These words of hers truly resonated with me."[64]

Christine describes how advocacy for those living with dementia would be her legacy, and it gave her an important source of self-worth. She became an advocate for persons living with dementia to be involved in dementia policy. She began connecting with other people living with dementia and began advocating for their voice to be heard at conferences and in science. "[A colleague] …told me that someone in the USA had read my book and was really keen to get in touch with me – would it be okay if she gave out my email address to this person? I said yes, of course. The person was Morris Friedell, an American sociology professor who also had dementia. His friend Laura Smith had set up an internet support group, which by the time Morris told me about it (2000) was called the Dementia Advocacy and Support Network (DASN) and would later add 'International' to its name to reflect its global reach. I was keen to join this group and got involved immediately – and I was introduced to a worldwide community I hadn't known was there. It was great to meet friends all over the world who had dementia. They were all like me – hoping to connect, willing

---

[64] Bryden, Christine. Before I Forget . Position 2155-2157 Penguin Books Ltd. Kindle Edition.

to speak out, wanting to challenge preconceived ideas about dementia and the people who have dementia. Suddenly I didn't feel like I was fighting the battle alone anymore."[65]

How to Leave This Legacy in a Time When Communication or Executive Function may be Impaired

We have discussed in previous chapters that, due to the effects of dementia, communication may be changing. Your ability to articulate or transcribe or create the story or legacy you'd like to pass along to family may be impaired. It is a time to obtain help – whether from a family member, friend, colleague, or a neighbor. To help stimulate stories, consider using props such as clothes, pictures, old addresses, etc. as in done in reminiscence or life review therapy. You can try lists of questions, but don't become stressed by the questions – just see if they trigger any interesting stories. Let the others in the room take the notes or video and then review the stories that arise. You should have final say on if the story was captured correctly and whether it needs further editing. The stories could also be fashioned into a creative piece, such as poetry or pictorial representation of your story.

It may be beneficial to make some short "story boards," books, or videos to share with family and paid caregivers in the future. Those who share stories allow for closer connection with their caregivers since they will understand more completely your personhood.

Don't have an extended family to assist you? Consider reaching out to a local college or nursing/social work/occupational

---

[65] Bryden, Christine. Before I Forget. Location 1928-1933. Penguin Books Ltd. Kindle Edition.

therapy school. Think broadly – consider colleges of journalism and public relations. Many work with individuals to tell their stories while teaching their students powerful lessons in humanity. In an article written about occupational therapy students at Quinnipiac College in Hamden Connecticut, the reciprocity in the telling and transcribing the story for both the teller and the scribe is evident. If no one in your area is doing something like this, use this example of the legacy project at Quinnipiac to spur them into action.[66]

Christine Bryden noticed things changing and adapted. "Naturally there were changes compared to my pre-dementia days. Back when I was working, I was able speak off the cuff to a handful of slides, about a whole range of complex issues relating to scientific research, but now when I give a talk I read out what I have prepared, word for word – like driving and like talking on the phone, reading aloud is a skill that I have painstakingly re-learned over the last few years. Even at the beginning of my advocacy, I used a rich and complex vocabulary – looking back on my talks of five to ten years ago, they have bigger words than I am now able to pronounce easily. These days my words are simpler and more direct. But I'm still here, still working, still thinking, still creating. In March 2011 we went to Toronto, and I did address the whole conference. I thought to myself, I'm back."[67]

I would like to finish this chapter with what I think I gleaned as Christine Bryden's legacy in the reading of her works, in her words!

---

66 https://www.qu.edu/magazine/book-project-unites-students-people-living-with-dementia

67 Bryden, Christine. Before I Forget . Position 2345-2350 Penguin Books Ltd. Kindle Edition

"I do think that my attitude to life and to dementia has helped me a lot. I choose to try to live positively. In so doing, I am making a journey into the center of self, away from the complex cognitive outer layer that once defined me, through the jumble and tangle of emotions created through my life experiences, into the centre of my being, into what gives me true meaning in life. This, I hope, will remain intact despite the ravages of dementia. I have chosen to be a dementia survivor, living life positively each day, with my enabler, Paul, alongside me. My attitude to life is positive – I am charging out of the trenches of despair, waving my tattered flag of effort and rehab. I will be bold; I will seize the moment; I will even try to excel. There's a drama to this survival, of hanging on and yet aiming high. I am celebrating my twenty-year survival, looking back over the roller-coaster ride it took to get there."[68]

Points to Remember

- Dr. Elizabeth Hunter says, "Legacy is making meaning of life. More than merely leaving behind a mark of some kind, or giving away one's possessions, legacy creation provided a means to fulfill the deeper need of creating a coherent end to the twists and turns of fate that typified each woman's life story."

- Erik Erickson, Ph.D., posits that the final stages of psycho-social development focus on generativity (vs. stagnation) and ego integrity (vs. despair). Generativity is the sense of "making your mark" on the world. addressing the questions

---

[68] Bryden, Christine. Before I Forget. Location 2623-2631 Penguin Books Ltd. Kindle Edition

of what are my accomplishments and what have I done to make the world a better place?

- The idea of the Legacy Link is to create an "ethical will," passing on the meaning of your life in the context of three generations before you and to affect three generations into the future. While much of legacy is often facts and figures, the legacy project asks us to consider the "why" of our legacy – why does it matter that we pass something along?

- Legacy can take many forms: a tangible keepsake, a story, photographs, audio or video recordings, letters, journals, jewelry or other possessions, books or texts, hobbies, special gifts or endowments, life lessons.

Action Plan

- Begin to think about what you would want to leave as your legacy. What creates a coherent story to the twist and turns of your life? It may not be the end yet, but can you think about what impact you'd like to leave and begin to live into it?

- Make a list of the potential ways you'd like to "make a mark" as Dr. Erikson discusses in his hierarchy of meaning.

- What is the "why" behind your legacy – how can you capture that?

- Explore the ideas for legacies offered in this book. Do any of them spark your interest? Do you need help putting something together? Who would you ask for help?

Resources

Christine Bryden, *Before I Forget*

In this memoir, Christine Bryden, a science writer and mother, describes her life once diagnosed with young-onset dementia (at age 46). At the time of the publication of her book, she had lived with dementia for 20 years. She describes her life before dementia, how she takes care of her brain health, what a day can be like, some of her setbacks and, most importantly, how having purpose has sustained her.

Viktor Frankl, *Man's Search for Meaning*

Written by Austrian neurologist-psychiatrist and Holocaust survivor Victor Frankl, this book is simple yet intense and reflective. Frankl is the founder of logotherapy, a form of existential psychology. Frankl narrates his personal experiences in the Auschwitz concentration camp to present an incredible concept: we can find purpose or meaning in any situation – even under the most horrendous conditions. Through descriptive illustrations of human condition, Frankl infuses hope into readers and encourages them to discover their own potential for resilience.

Chapter 6

REFLECTION

Overview

Why reflection? We want to live well now and establish the habits of living well for the moderate stages and the goals for the end stages. How do we do this?

A TED talk by Jake Barton[69] helps me articulate the importance of our stories. He quotes Anna Deavere Smith, who famously said that there's a literature inside of each of us. Mr. Barton has worked at StoryCorps, the Cleveland Museum of Art and the 9/11 Memorial and Museum. In all his projects, he and his team have found a way for a personal story to be woven throughout. It is that experience that I wish for your journey with dementia, that as you progress through the disease. I hope that you can leave your personal museum for the others in your life, to bring out the best of you. How will the people in your life know what you'd like them to know about you? How can you know? What aspect of you would you curate? In his talk, Barton

---

69 https://www.ted.com/talks/jake_barton_the_museum_of_you?language=en

shows a piece of the interaction in the Cleveland Museum where a face can be made by the visitor and a piece from the museum with some matching aspect of the face, for example – a similar smile, will be brought up digitally and a map to the piece so that the museum visitor can visit and explore that piece. Imagine if you left clues as to what would bring up some of your laughter, your tears, your tenderness, your sweetest memories. Can you leave a few StoryCorps moments – snippets of questions and answers? Barton describes them as an act of love, which is listening itself. Can you leave some etches that you feel would bring out something in you?

The Kenny Family Story

My mother used to puff her cheeks out in a silly way to indicate when she was full – too full for another bite. She did this before she had dementia, but it became her short-hand way to tell us to stop pushing food at her. And my kids would parrot it. And use that shorthand to connect and make her smile, make her feel heard and seen and respected. We still use that shorthand today, 10 years after my mother's death, sometimes at the Thanksgiving table, sometimes just for fun and to bring back happy memories of my mother. My mother always tried to find a playful way to get her uncomfortable communication across.

Why We Might Resist Reflection

You may not want to spend time addressing your own thoughts and why you may not want to think about death and dying, about dementia, about the loss of communication and your intellect. Lynn Casteel Harper, author of *On Vanishing*, is a chaplain living in New York City who has worked with people living with dementia. Her grandfather lived with and died from dementia, and she wrote a On Vanishing contemplating her feelings, society's feeling, and our feelings about dementia, addressing how many in society want those with dementia to vanish from our view. Ms. Harper challenges this vanishing by highlighting the famous passage from Ecclesiastes contrasting times for birth and death, building and tearing down, laughing and crying. You may know the passage as the words to the famous song, Turn! Turn! Turn! written by Pete Seeger and made famous by the Byrds in 1965 using the words from the King James' Bible passage.

"These lines in Ecclesiastes encourage readers to imagine a world in which the poles of existence create vibrant tension, in which life and death, gathering and releasing, embracing and refraining, weeping and laughing, do not negate each other, but instead balance and enrich. There is aggregation and integration – even with loss, even in death."

She goes on to point out, "Dementia, too, invites this kind of conjunction. There is dilution and distillation, constriction and expansion, disorder and constancy. Certain aspects of persons and their relationships fade – and other dimensions crystallize, possessing a new kind of clarity. Dementia places new constraints on communication – and relationships expand to include new ways of being and loving. Cognitive changes upset the usual patterns of one's life – and some rhythms remain unchanged."[70]

---

[70] Harper, Lynn Casteel. On Vanishing (pp. 18-19). Catapult. Kindle Edition

Strategies to Get You Going

Choose a time when the mind is as clear as possible. This is not a task for when someone is tired. Maybe it's after a gentle walk, one that has sparked your energy. Maybe it's with a cup of tea and the afternoon light coming through the window. Maybe it's the first thing in the morning when the world is quiet when there are not as many distracting sounds of the world and of people bustling off to work. Maybe it's on a park bench, where bird's song and sounds of children playing are your background music.

Use any medium. Written thoughts will be most easily understood by others, but if your communication style is something else, please use that. An audio recording? A video? A poem? A sculpture, painting, or etching? A cartoon? What moves you to reflect on your life and your wishes?

What are the questions? I've listed a few below to get you started. Please add more or choose only a few. The goal is to explore what you think – in a wonderful way, with curiosity, not with anxiety or dread. This is a time of opening, not shrinking. Open the corners of yourself that you may be afraid of and see what is there. You can always choose to edit those pieces back out after they have been explored.

Some questions may serve to reflect on your values – we will go over some of those more in the next chapter. Let's warm up our "reflection muscle" by addressing issues that may leave clues for those who will be assisting in our lives as we travel this road with dementia.

- How do I want to live?
    - What makes life meaningful or worthwhile?

REFLECTION

- ◊ How adaptable am I to alternatives to the images the first question revealed?
- ◊ How much am I willing to "pay" in inconvenience, suffering, or monetary value to create the life I imagine?
- What makes life unbearable? Can I imagine what this might look like?
- What comforts me when I'm lonely?
- What comforts me when I'm scared?
- What annoys me when I'm lonely or scared?
- How easily do I become bored?
- What causes boredom in me? Some people (introverts, for example) may become bored with chit-chat and socialization and need time alone or with a book. In contrast, an extrovert may become bored with reading a book and crave interaction to fight their boredom.
- How easily do I become overstimulated?
- How do I react when I am frustrated?
- How short is my fuse to anger – what triggers it and what calms it?

Use prompts. If you draw a blank when you review some of your questions, use a prompt to nudge your brain. In the next passage by Thomas DeBaggio, an individual living with Alzheimer's dementia and the author of several books, including *When It Gets Dark: An Enlightened Reflection on Life with Alzheimer's*, we find that he is open to some using a prompt to clarify his thoughts.

"I am delighted you have the old ration book. Objects make for much stronger ties to the past and can serve to release powerful memories. My fondest relic is the ticket that brought my grandfather to America. It was found in my grandmother's safe deposit box after she died a few years ago. Although Grandpa always said the food on the ship was lousy, the menu on the back of the ticket doesn't sound bad. Like most food, and much of life, reality sometimes rests between expectations and execution.[71]

This could be a clue to Tom's personal blueprint on adapting to something not meeting expectations. His care partners could tap into this story as a touchpoint for him in his future care. They may say, "Remember how Grandpa hated the food on the ship, but those menus didn't look so bad! Give it a try! It might not be so bad!" Tapping into this story may make the connection that Tom needs as a work-around to resistance to trying something due in his future care.

And through photographs and letters, DeBaggio is looking for memories of his grandmother who had just died at age 104. DeBaggio uses the photographs to reveal a complex time full of strife. He realizes that working in dirt, his garden, can move him to release pent-up emotions. This is a wonderful clue to a beautiful strategy for his self-care and for those who partner in his care.

"Kind, wonderful Joyce [his wife] handed me photographs and letters from a time my memory told me was a blistering emotional moment of moral torment, but the memories in these old boxes were not the chronicle of alienation I thought were

---

71 DeBaggio, Thomas. When It Gets Dark: An Enlightened Reflection on Life with Alzheimer's (p. 121). Free Press. Kindle Edition.

there. ……Only the earth and time have the power to restore stillness. This was a time before the earth reached up to me through my garden and said, yes, it is all right to cry."[72]

Consider using photographic or letter prompts to help you unfold your personal truths that may also help in understanding what will help you when you need soothing.

Reflections to Guide the Progression of the Disease

Going a bit deeper, can you begin to imagine how the progression of the disease may or may not change your thoughts on your wishes? This can be a difficult exercise, but focus on the question of "how do I want to live?" There will be changes and adaptations, but if we do not and cannot imagine the next stages, we cannot imagine the good that may be mixed with the more difficult. As a society, we shy away from the difficult, but there is great beauty, wonder, and surprise at the edges.

Early Stages

How do I want to live? My friends and I just had a conversation about this in a text exchange. We bounced ideas of what we would want if we all lived together in old age. We want someone to plan and drive us to a weekly outing (e.g., a play or a museum visit). The communal house would have a garden and reading room. We also wanted someone to read to us each afternoon, if our eyes were tired. The text went on and on. We opened ourselves to imagine what we really desired. Nothing was too grand ... although there was a hot tub mentioned. But each of us thought about what filled us – it was laughter, quiet,

---

[72] DeBaggio, Thomas. When It Gets Dark: An Enlightened Reflection on Life with Alzheimer's (p. 146). Free Press. Kindle Edition

learning, connecting, and exploring in various ways. What fills you? How do you want to see it show up in your life?

Thomas DeBaggio says, "Simple things count: a cat playing with a shadow cast by an open window, a piece of wild twine blowing on the windowsill."[73]

Please capture some of these small things that make a difference to you. Begin a log of them. They can be used by those in your life to make connections to you – the special you that lights you up or brings you to tears – to your humanity. I love Thomas DeBaggio's poetic and philosophical musings, which speak to all of our needs to change and adapt – whether we are living with dementia or we are not. "My early-morning walks may not have the thrill of a daybreak stroll through Rome, where it appears nothing is thrown away and everything remains as it has been for centuries, but the daily hike is more than a stroll down memory lane. I have come to realize my morning constitutional holds important remnants of comfort, anger, inquiry, wonder, bewilderment, and friendship. My walks offer all the things necessary for intelligent life. As my personal landmarks have begun to disappear, I have awakened to an unsettling side of the American character. Instead of preserving the mundane and ordinary from a past, we constantly demolish it, destroying the keys to our own and society's rich past and to an understanding of the present. The habitat of twentieth century America, polished by its residents with laughter and hardship, has begun to shift constantly, the American character."[74]

---

73 DeBaggio, Thomas. When It Gets Dark: An Enlightened Reflection on Life with Alzheimer's (p. 139). Free Press. Kindle Edition

74 DeBaggio, Thomas. When It Gets Dark: An Enlightened Reflection on Life with Alzheimer's (pp. 59-60). Free Press. Kindle Edition

Reflections on Change

The early stage of dementia is often about change. Take time to address how you handle change. Dementia comes into our lives when we have had some time on this planet. We probably have an idea how we've dealt with change. If you've rolled with change in the past, that's wonderful. Many of us don't. But can we begin to embrace change? Thomas DeBaggio tells a beautiful story of the importance of a tree in the choice of how to address change. Tom and his wife, Joyce, had newly purchased a house on Ash Street. The tree offered beauty, shade, and a home for birds and squirrels. With time, the tree began to decay and threaten the house. Tom called the town, and braced himself that the tree may need to be torn down, but it required only a trim. The tree remained for 20 more years, but then the town sent a notice that it would be removed, although the removal date was delayed 22 months. In that time, he and Joyce continued to enjoy the tree. The tree removal day came, and the debris from the stump was used as mulch for his garden. Although Tom and Joyce's beloved tree was no longer going to be in their life, the change brought something new and also beloved – nurturing for their garden.

"We took the proposed tree removal in stride, which was unusual because humans accept nothing and alter everything."[75]

I notice this in my life too … at first, I get upset that someone is changing "my" landscape in some way. But then I see it as inevitable, and I adjust and adapt and perhaps even enjoy the changes that comes!

---

75 DeBaggio, Thomas. When It Gets Dark: An Enlightened Reflection on Life with Alzheimer's (p. 150). Free Press. Kindle Edition

Reflections on the Practical

There is the practical: You have a voice. What is happening in the day-to-day that may need to be adapted? Thomas DeBaggio gives an excellent example of a side-effect from a medication. "Some mornings, after I take two Exelon tablets, I float away on a tranquil sea. It is an unwelcome feeling, and I cannot work efficiently until early afternoon. I mentioned the condition to Dr. Blanchfield, and she immediately cut my Exelon dose in half and began Aricept again, one tablet at night."[76]

When something is not working – a medication, a communication style, loss of function that needs help, someone taking away something that you still can do – make sure your voice is heard. Don't doubt or wonder or sit in worry. Take notes about what you notice. Bring it up so that you can find support in dealing with whatever the situation is and adjust or adapt. Just as Tom did regarding the floating away feeling caused by his medication.

Moderate Stages

What may happen in the more moderate stages of dementia? Many of the authors you meet in this book will talk about some of the changes that disturb them. DeBaggio has his dark thoughts, including his preoccupation with death, scattered throughout his memoir. "There are days full of static when little memory remains, and I wander over the hidden landscape like a child trying to catch slippery raindrops. The interior cacophony I carry within me is full of broken sentences, and tears. There are other days when memory is so thick and beautiful, I can't

---

[76] DeBaggio, Thomas. When It Gets Dark: An Enlightened Reflection on Life with Alzheimer's (p. 58). Free Press. Kindle Edition.

see the world for all the happy congestion. So, this is the way my world ends, fighting shadows, wrapped in fear, trembling to remember who I am and where I am headed. Despite the poverty of words, and a memory chewed by Alzheimer's, I intend to open my inner life and at the same time reflect on everyday simple things, as death's shadow falls across my dwindling days. This is not a book of kings and queens but of ordinary people struggling in the world they inhabit. It is my world, and the world of my wife, Joyce, and son, Francesco. This is not a book crafted with care and threaded with hope. It is a book of anger and tears, expressed in a cage of waiting death ruled by Alzheimer's, a disease without survivors. I became a creature of the tension between a life of the moment and the languid, rotting fruit of memory upon which I rely for life. This is not a book barren of trees, birds and ordinary sweat. In the end, this book is about becoming silent, while all around cars honk impatiently."[77]

Preparing for the Moderate Stages

The people living with dementia discuss confusion, fatigue, frustration and bewilderment.

"I didn't understand the images on the screen. I didn't have a clue how to write the check, something I had done regularly for years. I was in tears before I asked Joyce [his wife] for help, and she explained everything and got the check printed. I trembled with anger and bewilderment when I got to the bank. Some of the tellers at the bank are unaware of my mental illness and look at me with bewilderment sometimes. The bank is now one

---

[77] DeBaggio, Thomas. When It Gets Dark: An Enlightened Reflection on Life with Alzheimer's (p. 5). Free Press. Kindle Edition.

of the places I avoid if I can. It was another reminder of how far along I have walked on the path with Alzheimer's."[78]

As adults, we know that all of life is full of confusion, fatigue, frustration, and bewilderment, but with waning cognitive function, the quantity and the shape of these experiences may be heightened or take on atypical characteristics. Finally, our usual ability to cope independently may be lost.

The words of authors living with dementia also leave clues to what soothes. What we know is that each of us is unique – what works for Sally may not work for Bob. I ask you to reflect on what soothes you.

Let's leave a road map. Use some of these prompts to scour your life experiences for what may be helpful when you feel frustrated or bewildered by your disease or life.

Senses

Sounds – There is a host of literature on the soothing effects of natural sounds, music, and nature and the boost to health. The multi-dimensional experience of being in nature may be even more powerful, as nature will add sights, smells, and possibly ionic stabilization. There is still much to learn, but historically, healers knew to add birdsong, gardens, and running water sounds to environments that bring about health/healing and to avoid loud, disconsonant noises that are jarring and unnerving.[79]

---

78 DeBaggio, Thomas. When It Gets Dark: An Enlightened Reflection on Life with Alzheimer's (pp. 69-70). Free Press. Kindle Edition

79 Franco LS, Shanahan DF, Fuller RA. A Review of the Benefits of Nature Experiences: More Than Meets the Eye. Int J Environ Res Public Health. 2017 Aug 1;14(8):864. doi: 10.3390/ijerph14080864. PMID: 28763021; PMCID: PMC5580568.

REFLECTION

"By nightfall, those morning thoughts often appear silly and surreal, but it is good to recall them because they are part of the day's reality. The conflict between the tender, hopeful glow of the morning and the anxiety of the hard, dark evening is healed in the garden, where opposites are resolved in activity delighting mind and body."[80]

Smells – "As I stood with a hose in my hand watering lavenders, a familiar scent came to me. It was not a sweet herbal aroma, nor a scent from the donut shop down the street. It was a scent bringing the past and all its memories with a rush. I don't know how to explain such a scent without sounding foolish or mystical. I can say this much: it was a complex perfume of Prince Albert pipe tobacco, hard work, old clothes, and the kitchen aromas of frying meat, steam rising from boiling vegetables, gravy, and baking pies. The scent that reached my nose was the distinct, remembered aroma of my grandfather, born of restaurant kitchens, his pipe and the Midwest farming town of Eldora, Iowa, where he lived. It was as if he were next to me, looking over my shoulder, and I turned involuntarily first to my left and then to my right, half expecting him to be there. There was no one; my grandfather has been dead for years. Grandpa's aroma was in the air around this spot in the garden all morning and I walked around it and through it. The scent was the same each time, and it brought back a flood of memories."[81]

I love this passage. We know that scent can be powerful in evoking memory. Scents bypass the thalamus and go straight to the brain's smell center, known as the olfactory bulb. The

---

80 DeBaggio, Thomas. When It Gets Dark: An Enlightened Reflection on Life with Alzheimer's (p. 62). Free Press. Kindle Edition.
81 DeBaggio, Thomas. When It Gets Dark: An Enlightened Reflection on Life with Alzheimer's (p. 100). Free Press. Kindle Edition.

olfactory bulb is directly connected to the amygdala and hippocampus, which might explain why the smell of something can so immediately trigger a detailed memory or even intense emotion. Use this knowledge to help you uncover memories to help in your reflection.

Touch/Proprioception – Research suggests that the sense of touch plays a fundamental role in human communication and even physical health. Hugging is beneficial in many ways. It can help to reduce stress, show care and concern for someone else, and trigger the release of the hormone oxytocin, which promotes happiness. Moreover, hugging is linked to health benefits like alleviating symptoms of illness and enhancing blood circulation. According to research, receiving a five-minute hand massage can trigger a physical relaxation response and decrease the presence of cortisol, a hormone that is released during periods of stress. Additionally, massage has been shown to increase levels of serotonin, a neurotransmitter that promotes relaxation and lessens anxiety.

Expand your thoughts on touch. What do you think of bedding? For me, I enjoy cool sheets, but not silky. I like my blankets soft but not heavy. There is research that promotes the use of weighted blankets. Weighted blankets have been found to be helpful for improving various stress-related conditions such as sleep, fatigue, depression, anxiety, and physiologic stress in adults with mental health disorders.

Sights – What to look at? I know I will ask for a clear aesthetic – I cannot look at too much without becoming unsettled. Many would think my home too stark or too plain. My mother-in-law has a more comfy, filled home. I know, if she were to need care, to fill her visual field with a stream of quaint, soft, warm sights and colors.

Thomas DeBaggio leaves clues in his writings. "Even with its unkempt appearance, the garden's plants shine with brilliance. The silver lavender foliage floats above the underbrush of weeds like silver clouds."[82]

Ms. Casteel mentions a client in one of her spiritual groups. "Far from disengaged, Vera always appeared alert and intent, making eye contact with me and other group members. If we gave her ample time, she would offer a word or two to the discussion. When the group learned that she loved cats, we began to incorporate feline-themed pictures and poems into our meetings, which made Vera smile. I remember her son's shock when he visited from out of town and found his mother participating in the group."[83]

Tastes – Oh, for me, there is not a taste I would turn away from! But, if I had to choose my absolute favorite taste, it would be cold and creamy. This I adopted from my mother! There is not a cone, dish, sundae, cake, or pie that is not made better by ice cream. If anyone wonders how to make me calm or happy in my future, it will be ice cream. The only thing better would be if I could share the experience with another who also enjoys that same taste!

Is there a taste that brings a sense of calm or home? Many of us consider food as comfort. Is it milk and cookies? The earthy goodness of mushrooms? The sweet pop of berries off the vine?

---

82 DeBaggio, Thomas. When It Gets Dark: An Enlightened Reflection on Life with Alzheimer's (p. 80). Free Press. Kindle Edition
83 Harper, Lynn Casteel. On Vanishing (pp. 89-90). Catapult. Kindle Edition.

I had a patient who would lose weight each winter and spring, but I learned not to worry too much, as each summer into fall, he would be so taken with his tomato crop (which he ate with bacon, bread, lettuce, and mayo), that he would put on the pounds he lost as he had less appetite without fresh tomatoes!

Environment

Technically, this can be about our senses – I realize that. But what I am getting at here is more about the bigger picture of the energy of the compilation of the sights, sounds, etc. that make the environment.

As processing the sights and sounds and people and activities can become overwhelming, what does quiet time away look like? Thomas DeBaggio offers this reflection: "There are days filled with languid time in which a vacation-attitude prevails. I thumb through magazines and investigate fishing rod catalogs when I should be working, but I cannot push my dreams away long enough to begin scribbling. I prefer to live in this make-believe world of soft air-conditioned breezes where everything is perfect and without frustration. Alone in this room, no one sees whether I am working or playing, and it is easy to become someone else in this hidden place of imagination. I am a little boy again, hiding in a box, dreaming of the impossible, the unbelievable."[84]

He needed to be allowed to relax and daydream – but with the illusion of productivity. I know this sounds crazy, but it's real! We have all been conditioned to use our time productively! I

---

84 DeBaggio, Thomas. When It Gets Dark: An Enlightened Reflection on Life with Alzheimer's (p. 72). Free Press. Kindle Edition.

live with a chronic disease, and when it flares, I need more rest. Sometimes it is hard to justify this rest, and I become hard on myself. I've learned to hear that harsh voice, thank it for its concern, and relax into my need to take a break.

What works for you regarding this energy flow of your life? What do you need ...

Change? Things to remain steady? Are you easily bored? Do you love or hate a routine? What helps you ... and for how long?

Naps – do you wake up refreshed or wake up groggy? What helps you wake up?

Please leave some clues for those who may assist in directing your days.

Preparing for the End Stage

"In life there are sweet and glorious revelations every day, but the deep secrets hidden by death, especially that of a relative or dear friend, remain unknown and as mysterious as the fog."[85]

This quote by Tom DeBaggio is fitting. There is mystery in death. We will not be able to plan it. We will not know what is to come.

But that is not a reason to ignore it. Lynn Casteel Harper begins *On Vanishing* at the Metropolitan Museum of Art and an exhibit of still-life painting in the *vanitas* method. "It involves carefully juxtaposing objects deemed symbolic of life's brevity and the evanescence of earthly achievements. Objects such as mirrors, broken or tipped glassware, books, decaying flowers,

---

[85] DeBaggio, Thomas. When It Gets Dark: An Enlightened Reflection on Life with Alzheimer's (p. 143). Free Press. Kindle Edition.

and skulls are meant to encourage viewers to contemplate their own mortality."[86]

As Harper introduces us to her ideas, she reminds us that contemplating the brevity of our lives is important when we are fully alive. It gives us the context to make meaning of our here and now. It reminds us that we all have an end, a thought that many of us push to the back corners of our thinking.

She goes on to note, "To be human is to be limited, even in our most cherished capacities. Perhaps more than other conditions, dementia brings our fundamental lack of ultimate control over our lives, and their endings, to a head."[87]

I have heard many people living with dementia find freedom from this thought. I was just in a group session in which all 6 people agreed that the diagnosis of dementia had provided them with the 'gift' of reconsidering their lives in a new way. Being diagnosed with dementia focused the participants attention to the way they are living their lives and allowed them to reimagine and redirect their activities.

"In life, as in the garden, the dark secret of unpredictable death puzzles and bewilders, intrigues and frightens. Everyone reaches to touch the newborn child and hold its promise of young, long life, but at the same time, we wish the elderly out of sight; their wrinkles and infirmities remind us of what awaits for them and for us."[88]

The words of DeBaggio ring true. But, only from a society viewpoint. The group participants I described above are

---

86 Harper, Lynn Casteel. On Vanishing (pp. 3-4). Catapult. Kindle Edition.
87 Harper, Lynn Casteel. On Vanishing (pp. 5-6). Catapult. Kindle Edition.
88 DeBaggio, Thomas. When It Gets Dark: An Enlightened Reflection on Life with Alzheimer's (p. 143). Free Press. Kindle Edition.

choosing not to focus on their wrinkles and infirmities, but on what they have left.

What do you want ... we will dive deeper in the Values chapter but wanted to begin the Reflections chapter first. To whet our appetite for questioning what we want and what we value. These reflections need to be repeated, to dive deeper, past our first thoughts, which often give a hasty reply to brush away this task. It may be difficult, but those that pay attention to their reflections are happier, and their families are better adjusted.

Questions to Contemplate for the Late Stages of Dementia:

- What does it mean to you to have your family care for you?
- Does the idea of family caring for you give you comfort? If not, why not?
- Is there a type of care you would prefer to be done by someone other than a family member?
- What is your most important concern? Safety? Calm? Connection? What would you be willing to sacrifice to have this?
- How flexible are you in having someone else modify your wishes?

As you state these wishes, be brave enough to see that how the carer feels will be coming into play as well. Your life will become more of a dance and interplay with the one who will be your primary care partner. In the late stage of dementia, their needs will now be interlaced with yours. You may give guidance, but it must be interpreted within their needs, wants, and complex background as well.

You may have several individuals assisting you in your journey with dementia. I hope that you do! Likely though, there will be one person who makes the majority of the day-to-day decisions. They will need to prepare for this aspect of your journey as it will become a journey of we; me and another; me and a family. The discussion you will be having with them, as you reflect and sort your values will be helpful. Consider recommending to them that they share reading this book with you. In that way, you can openly discuss how their needs, wants and complex background can be addressed within your requests for care.

Remember that they may find great joy and meaning in serving you – so while your concern may be for their burden, they may not see loving and caring for you as a burden. Discussion will likely include where you would like your care delivered, if all things go according to plans.

You may wish to remain at home for your care, but if your care takes on intense complexity, as it may be due to an unknown situation, the best care may be in a facility allowing your family member to provide emotional and spiritual support, more than hands-on care. These situations are best discussed with an individual that will be intimately involved in this decision.

Dr Jack Kevorkian, also known as Dr Death, was a physician who supported euthanasia and performed 130 assisted deaths during the 1990's, was convicted of manslaughter and spent 8 years in jail. I believe the story that Harper imagines of Dr. Kevorkian's first patient, Janet Adkins, allows us an insight into the complex interplay between one with dementia and their care partner. Dr. Kevorkian's first patient was a woman living with early-stage dementia who chose physician-assisted death relatively early in her journey with dementia. "Ron Adkins publicly voiced support for his wife's decision, but I wonder if he helped with her not to do it – that it might be his honor to be burdened by her. Perhaps he resented his wife's determination that he should not be asked to do so. Perhaps he could come up with nothing more pressing in his life that would render caring for his wife a lesser good. Perhaps he was willing to risk their futures. He had purchased his wife a round-trip ticket; in case she changed her mind and wished to return to Oregon with him. I have witnessed many loving partners unable to rise to the occasion – and perhaps this is what Janet Adkins wished to avoid. I have seen one spouse keep the other alive in any means necessary because the idea of being without the person is simply unbearable. Maybe Janet Adkins knew that love is blindness at times. Maybe the only person she trusted was herself, in the present – and a pathologist in Michigan."[89]

How to Reflect

Writing – this is how DeBaggio did it. He had an editor, Linda Ligon, who, he writes, pushed him to look deeply. Could I be that person now, asking you to look deeply?

"It was my good fortune several years ago to cross paths with Linda Ligon, as fine a friend and word maven as I have met. She surprised me one day with a gift: praise for my scribbles and a chance to share them with others. Later, she pushed

---

89   Harper, Lynn Casteel. On Vanishing (pp. 36-38). Catapult. Kindle Edition.

me to poke in simple but dirty places, where I found overlooked meaning."[90]

But to look deeply, we must be well tended to. It's like the passage that Tom DeBaggio borrows from Charles Dudley Warner, author of A Summer in the Garden, about a sunset being so precious. "I know that a sunset is commonly looked on as a cheap entertainment; but it is really one of the most expensive. It is true that we can all have front seats, and we do not exactly need to dress for it as we do for the opera; but the conditions under which it is to be enjoyed are rather dear. Among them I should name a good suit of clothes. ... I should also add a good dinner, well-cooked and digestible; and the cost of a fair education, extended, perhaps, through generations in which sensibility and love of beauty grew. What I mean is, that if a man is hungry and naked and half a savage, or with the love of beauty undeveloped in him, a sunset is thrown away on him: so that it appears that the conditions of the enjoyment of a sunset are as costly as anything in our civilization."[91]

What does it take to be prepared to think deeply about how you would want the end of a disease to play out when you may no longer have a say? There are choices. Letting the disease play out without having a say is one choice. We will discuss what this typically looks like in below in the medical aspects of choices.

There are other choices too. What if you put some thought into these ... what if you stay with me to see how this could go

---

90 DeBaggio, Thomas. Position 30 When It Gets Dark: An Enlightened Reflection on Life with Alzheimer's . Free Press. Kindle Edition.
91 DeBaggio, Thomas. When It Gets Dark: An Enlightened Reflection on Life with Alzheimer's (pp. 120-121). Free Press. Kindle Edition.

if you put some thought into these "dirty places" as DeBaggio mentions?

What would help? I propose we untangle this by looking at the medical, the psychological and the spiritual aspects of poking around. I can handle the medical and will fumble through, with the help of other authors, the psychological and spiritual.

Medically

I can give you the facts. There is a point in time when one shifts from living with dementia to dying from dementia. Medically, that time comes, whether we understand that shift or not. Many medical personnel do not know when that shift occurs. I believe many family members do not recognize it, but when they do, it changes choices. I believe, from watching so many people with dementia, that the person living with dementia often does recognize the change and begins to allow that death to occur. Unfortunately, the medical system, American culture, and often grieving families will stand in the way of allowing dying.

Here are some of the facts. Making an accurate assessment of prognosis is difficult in advanced dementia, but using a global deterioration scale, research shows that once profound memory deficits, minimal verbal ability, inability to walk independently, inability to care for daily activities, and incontinence of bowel and bladder have developed, average survival time is a little over a year. When the decline has reached this level, family and caregivers often opt for and value focusing on comfort rather than on survival.

There are common maladies that, if recognized and accepted, will allow for a relatively predictable and natural death. The difficulties that result from the deteriorating brain include inability or ineffective swallowing, leading to choking and allowing food and saliva into the lungs, and ineffective bladder contraction, which then causes bacterial growth in the urinary tract. These two situations lead to infections. Finally, the drive to eat is lost, for a host of reasons, and a person living with dementia naturally begins to eat less and less or, commonly, merely closes their mouth to food. The body knows when to do this. Unfortunately, the medical system or the family may begin to supplement, cajole, or force food. The excess food fights the natural death and can result in stomach aches, vomiting, or discomfort.

Psychologically

What do you think about how you address your own mortality? How can we address this better or assuage our concerns? Practice honestly.

I find this *New York Times* article, "Why Talking About Our Problems Helps So Much (and How to Do It)" by Eric Ravenscraft, helpful with logical tips (April 3, 2020).[92] Just naming an issue will diffuse the emotion about it and help move the conversation or thoughts in a productive direction. Find someone (or more than one someone) to discuss this difficult topic with as a sounding board. Choose wisely! Find someone who will support you, but who will not divert the conversation to commiseration. Also, choose someone who has the courage to listen and reflect, and not tell you that you shouldn't think about the end stages. During the time of supporting my mother, I saw a therapist, and found the experience to be wonderful for my mental health, clarity, and emotional regulation. I asked my mother to see a therapist earlier in her diagnosis of dementia as

---

92   https://www.nytimes.com/2020/04/03/smarter-living/talking-out-problems.html

REFLECTION

well. The therapist assisted her in coping with the diagnosis, to provide support and hope, and to discuss, openly and candidly, her thoughts about the end of her journey. It helped that her first discussions were not with me, someone she wanted to protect. She could practice what she wanted to say with the therapist, and that in turn helped our discussions so that I understood what she wanted.

I love the advice in the *New York Times* article to give yourself an endpoint. Whether you talk about this uncomfortable topic or write about it in a journal, it is important to do so in small bursts. Come back and read what you've written to see if it rings true. Modify and expand. Go deeper. When you feel you've captured your information, be sure to stop. Once you've captured what you feel about the end, it is time to get back to living! The purpose of this exercise is to help your family prepare and to obtain the end, as much as any of us can, that you would prefer. The exercise is meant to be freeing – to allow you to prepare and hopefully avoid the dread and worry for the end-stages with a plan. The plan then allows you to focus on the living now, making the most of the life that is immediately before you. Those who do this planning are reported to have a better quality of life. That is the goal.

Lynn Casteel Harper has some insights into the psychosocial aspects of dementia progression. "Kitwood [author of *Dementia Reconsidered: The Person Comes First and Proponent for a Personhood Approach to Dementia*] a prominent advocate for dementia argued that as the degree of neurological impairment increases, the person's need for psychosocial care increases. What traditionally happens is the exact opposite. As the degree of neurological impairment increases, the person becomes increasingly neglected and isolated, further increasing neurological impairment – a vicious circle. Malignant social psychology hastens the vanishing point." I think by opening conversations with family and friends, we can begin to counter this malignant social psychology – in fact, I think we must. Taking the time to reflect and discuss your needs and wants for the end of life with dementia will be the beginning swell against this malignant social psychology.

Here are some comments by Thomas DeBaggio as he is taking some time to reflect. "This is a familiar place, but I am told I have never been here. Was it in a dream I walked in this wet sand? Was this a forgotten moment of childhood? Far away the same ocean water wets the sky. A young mother lifts her laughing, naked baby in and out of the gentle waves. Hurrying water laps firm wet sand in the afternoon as death plays in my body. Time is now quickly forgotten, and memory is gone. There is only now. There is romance in a slow death, but like so much romance, it is not worth the trouble."[93]

I love Thomas DeBaggio's honesty and courage as he looks at the bittersweetness of his experience while contemplating his current life.

Spiritually

Spirituality can be broadly understood, but a basic definition of spirituality is feeling united with something greater than oneself. In the past, mental health professionals would often shy away from addressing religious or spiritual beliefs in therapy sessions. However, recent research has demonstrated that

---

93 DeBaggio, Thomas. When It Gets Dark: An Enlightened Reflection on Life with Alzheimer's (p. 43). Free Press. Kindle Edition.

faith-based and spiritual convictions contribute to psychological stability as well as physical well-being. Spiritual therapy is a form of counseling that attempts to treat a person's soul as well as mind and body by accessing individual belief systems and using that faith in a higher power to explore areas of conflict in life. People who believe in a guiding higher power may find spiritual therapy helps them achieve a deeper connection with this power. This form of therapy includes activities such as communing with nature, meditating, listening to music, and engaging in other non-traditional healing practices – all aimed at unifying the body and mind with one's soul. The ultimate objective is to delve into our innermost being for personal development. Although spirituality is frequently associated with religion, one's spiritual path may have nothing to do with a specific faith. Rather, it can refer to the acknowledgment of an individual's relationship to the universe around them. Many who identify as spiritual strive for harmony between themselves and their surroundings through engaging in spiritual therapy activities in order to reach this desired balance.

Spirituality and religion are critical sources of strength for many people, are the bedrock for finding meaning in life, and can be instrumental in promoting healing and well-being. There is growing evidence that spiritual values and behaviors improve physical and psychological well-being. Exploring these values can integrate and enhance the other work that you are doing to find answers in this time of reflection. Like any other potential source of meaning, religious faith or spirituality seems most authentic and valuable when it enables us to become as fully human as possible. It can help us get in touch with our own powers of thinking, feeling, deciding, willing, and acting.

The Dalai Lama teaches that religious beliefs are but one level of spirituality, and he makes reference to basic spiritual values, which include qualities of goodness, kindness, love, compassion, tolerance, forgiveness, human warmth, and caring.[94]

If you are lucky enough to have side-stepped life's "slings and arrows," as Shakespeare has called them,[95] engaging a spiritual counselor may be warranted. A spiritual counselor is someone who attends to a person who feels as though they need help in their spiritual life. These are specially trained imams, rabbis, priests, etc., who have a background in psychology. This sort of interaction is also sometimes referred to as pastoral counseling. If you practice a religion, you likely can find a spiritual counselor in your religious institution. If you do not, there are pastoral counselors on the Psychology Today site.[96]

How do we address the deep and existential questions of the impact of this disease on our life and what it means at the end? These are deep waters. Many of us have not waded into waters as deep, because we've led lives that have been protected or blessed or lucky. Others know these waters too well from other hardships that have come their way over the course of their lives.

Questions to Address When Considering Your Spirituality:

- Can someone guide you through your thoughts about your values and how they impact your interaction with your disease?

---

94 Dalai Lama. (2001). An open heart: Practicing compassion in everyday life. Boston: Brown Little.
95 Shakespeare's play Hamlet. In act 3, scene 1
96 https://www.psychologytoday.com/us/therapists/spirituality

- Are there spiritual texts that can help you in your reflection?

Some of us find spiritual connection in the form of pets, family, or friends.

Thomas DeBaggio comments throughout his book how his cat, Sabina, was with him during some of his dark times and when he didn't want to share these feelings with anyone.

"When I close my eyes at night, white klieg lights sweep my shut eyes with a blinding brilliance. The light is steady and pointed directly at me, illuminating an emptiness as large as a desert. I wonder whether this bright white light is searching for something or someone who is lost. My cat Sabina continues to guard me each night from a place on my bed, as she has since the word Alzheimer's entered my vocabulary."[97]

Lynn Casteel Harper has thoughts that end-stage may be the truest of our humanness. "The mystics might say what is left is a truer, purer self. The dissolving of all doing, the stripping away of the *vita activa* [the active life or active engagement], makes straight the path for the naked, beloved self to emerge. The deconstruction of ego can facilitate a new freedom of being."[98]

Final Thoughts on Reflection

I would like to end this section on reflection with some final words by Thomas DeBaggio in answer to his own question to himself, "Why do I garden?" And what he has learned about gardening as a reflection of life – to celebrate life every day!

---

97 DeBaggio, Thomas. When It Gets Dark: An Enlightened Reflection on Life with Alzheimer's (p. 56). Free Press. Kindle Edition
98 Harper, Lynn Casteel. On Vanishing (p. 36). Catapult. Kindle Edition.

"I have always distrusted insight appearing as if it were a natural element. There it purred in the sun like a fat, happy cat: gardening is a way to transcend everyday life. It is a crazy thought, even for a guy who threw away his dog-eared catechism 40 years ago when he broke ranks with the regiment. ... Now, here I was, a son of these people of the soil, in my backyard, tall and glorious, with my feet planted on hard Virginia clay, twitching with the idea that gardening is a means to transcend everyday life. Gardening may become a transcending experience, but it does not transcend life. Gardening is as necessary as thinking and breathing because it is a reflection of life. Gardening teaches it is not necessary to transcend everyday life. Gardening exists to celebrate life every day."[99]

Points to Remember

- Now is the time to collect the stories from your life to foster connection and to prepare to help those who will partner in your care know what to do and how to do it.
- This time of reflection can ground you in meaning and value so that facing the question of "What would I want my life to be like as I proceed through this disease?" is possible.
- Facing the idea of how you would like to die sets you up beautifully to consciously examine how you want to live today and as you progress through dementia.
- A framework may be helpful in these reflections. Examine your choices holistically. Evaluating the medical, psychosocial,

---

[99] DeBaggio, Thomas. When It Gets Dark: An Enlightened Reflection on Life with Alzheimer's (p. 117). Free Press. Kindle Edition

and spiritual aspects of the progression of dementia allows for a comprehensive viewpoint.

Action Plan

- Begin to carve out some time to reflect – for some a "holy" hour each day (or "holy" 15 minutes!), for others an end (or beginning) of the week special time.
- Choose a time when you find your mind is most clear. Morning? After exercise?
- Choose your modality – writing, video, sculpture. Use this chapter as a guide but record some clues to help those who help you or are left without you. Use prompts (e.g., questions or sensory stimulation) to activate remembrance and clarify factors that soothe you.
- Use the prompts in this chapter to begin to explore your wishes for living with dementia and to gather information to assist others in ensuring those wishes are honored. The wishes and clues need to be documented in some way to be of help later in your disease.

Resources

Thomas DeBaggio, When It Gets Dark: An Enlightened Reflection on Life with Alzheimer's.

The book is a mix of musing about DeBaggio's life as an early journalist and then as an herb farmer. It describes his thoughts and dreams as he shapes his life. Interspersed are the poetry, fear, frustration and anger he feels about Alzheimer's disease and how it is affecting him. This book was chosen for the reflection chapter because of the raw juxtaposition of DiBaggio's love for the life he has created with his fear and anger toward the disease and how it is affecting his life.

Lynn Casteel Harper, On Vanishing: Mortality, Dementia, and What It Means to Disappear.

Lynn Casteel Harper is a minister, chaplain, and essayist. This book is a beautifully written exploration of what it means to have dementia, especially in the United States, where the focus on independence and individuality are glorified. She explores language and cultural perspectives on vanishing in relation to having dementia. She uses stories of her grandfather, the individuals she serves as a chaplain in a long-term care facility and her contemplation as she has a genetic risk factor for dementia.

Chapter 7

VALUES

The Kenny Family Story

We are a lucky clan. The Kennys have had their ups-and-downs, like everyone, but we are lucky/blessed/fortunate that we were raised with a good sense that basing your decisions on values was the right way forward. Mind you, we didn't always take the right way forward, but with the breadcrumbs of having reflected on the values, we could find our way back!

Our parents spoke of their values and strongly held beliefs at the dinner table. They lived their values in their day-to-day lives. One of their key values was fiscal responsibility. My father, who lived with and died from cardiac disease at a relatively young age, made career and life-insurance decisions to ensure that his wife and family would be cared for if he should die young.

My mother, widowed in her early 50s, remarried in her early 70s. She made it clear that she wanted her second husband and her finances to be separate for their potential care needs and to support their respective "first families" as they aged. Mom had a prenuptial agreement drawn up and proceeded with the wedding. About eight years into the marriage, both my mother and her second husband started to show signs of cognitive loss. My mom knew that she and her husband would likely need some type of long-term care. She and her husband discussed what this would mean to each of them financially and they expanded their discussion to family and then legal counsel. She was told that if she and/or her husband required skilled nursing care, the prenuptial agreement would not protect their "separate" money, but rather, either one of their savings would be spent on the other. Their only financial protection would be a divorce.

This put my mother into a values quandary! Her core beliefs were in the teachings of her church, the sanctimony of marriage, and fiscal responsibility and family loyalty.

She took the information she was given and contacted more than one Catholic priest for guidance on the views of the church in her situation. She and her husband ultimately decided on a divorce to protect each of their respective families from being financially burdened if all savings went to caring for one individual rather than each of them. She and her husband remained "married in the eyes of the Church," and she was able to keep that commitment.

This was a difficult time for my mother but having strong values and being clear on them helped her know who to speak to and how to use the guidance of the lawyers and the clergy for her best way forward.

Why Values?

When we focus on our values, we know how we want to live. Further, there is increasing evidence that once you have identified your values, there are interventions that strengthen those values to improve and expand your quality of life in the face of chronic disease.

In many studies, clarity on values and character strengths have been associated with better emotion regulation, protection against the effects of stress, and a lower frequency of mental health concerns such as anxiety and depression. Persons who practice gratitude, forgiveness, and spirituality may be less likely to become clinically depressed. Those who cultivate character strengths lead psychologically healthier lifestyles.

While there are no studies specific to those living with dementia, evidence suggests that individuals with other chronic illnesses benefit from value and character strengths-based interventions for improving psychological well-being. Notably, positive interventions aimed at cultivating hope have shown some efficacy in improving quality of life and reducing symptoms of depression in populations with neurological disorders.[100]

Positive psychology posits that embracing all aspects of living with difficult life experiences, such as navigating a terminal illness, benefits well-being and may be a source of inspiration. Studies suggest well-being is best achieved by transforming struggles or the "dark side" of life to positives.

Peter Berry is a gentleman living with cognitive loss who advocated for dementia via bike rides and authoring a book.

---

[100] Lai ST, Lim KS, Low WY, Tang V. Positive psychological interventions for neurological disorders: A systematic review. Clin Neuropsychol. 2019 Apr;33(3):490-518. doi: 10.1080/13854046.2018.1489562. Epub 2018 Jun 24. PMID: 29938575.

Deb Bunt, co-author with Peter Berry of *Slow Puncture*, was extremely impressed by how Peter could ride and navigate on the bike rides, even as he was noticing more trouble with functioning in other aspects of his life. On his first ride across Britain ("Aberystwyth in Wales as my starting point (and not just because it was impossible to say and to spell!) and Aldeburgh in my beloved Suffolk as my finishing point." He argued it was more interesting than A to Z), he arranged everything – all the logistics. He knew he functioned best when he was up for a challenge, so he created challenges in his life. This was a value and a preference he had held all his life. So, he found someone to begin to ride with him, as he stopped trusting that he could safely ride alone – not that he didn't know he could ride but, he reasoned, if he had a bad cognitive day, the friend could get him home. Deb Bunt became that friend and assisted him in writing his book – he knew he could no longer read or write, but he could tell a good story and she could record it for him. She also was able to help him actualize his next adventures. Deb, who worried at times that he would not be able to handle the press that these adventures drew, was always astonished that after a long, hard day of cycling, he could articulate his story and advocate for persons living with dementia without difficulty, while she just wanted to sleep.

Put Simply – How do YOU Want to Live?

The work that we've done thus far is to ask very specifically, how do you want to live?

This work you've done, identifying stories, sensations, things that comfort you, the time/money/attention you want to put toward your legacy – all of that is so that you can distill beyond prestige, ego, keeping up with the Joneses, obligation, expectation to what you want – will assist in defining how you'd like to live.

What Matters to You?

John O'Donohue, writer, philosopher, expert in Celtic mystics, and poet, wrote often of his values. John Quinn is a journalist and Irish radio personality who compiled and published *Walking in Wonder*, an assortment of John O'Donohue's interviews and lectures, after his early death. In Quinn's introduction to the book, he states, "Wonder, imagination, and possibility were John's great concerns, and he articulated them in his own inimitable lyrical style." This you will see in O'Donohue's values as I select his quotes throughout this chapter.

For example, O'Donohue says, "One of the great places of wonder is inspiration. The lovely thing about the concept of wonder is that it completely escapes the grid of control and predictability. It seems to witness to another sense of sourcing which cannot be programmed which can be expected and which is always received with surprise."[101] This is a beautiful example of O'Donohue's values shaping his interpretation of the world as a better place. Peter Berry, too, shapes what he sees in the world by his viewing through his lens as a "warrior." Berry imbues his days with joy and meaning as a warrior.

Your Values as A Guide to Living Your Best Life

It can be tough to figure out what steps to take when faced with so many choices and so much change. That's where values come in. Values are the things that matter most to us,

---
101 O'Donohue, John. *Walking in Wonder*. p. 19.

the guiding principles that help us through tough times and make us who we are. By taking a "values inventory," we can get a better sense of what's important to us and use that knowledge to make decisions about how we want to live our lives and navigate any difficult decisions or transitions more mindfully on a day-to-day basis. Having a clearly defined set of ethics and beliefs will also provide clarity as you review your life successes, setbacks, losses, and triumphs – allowing you to both celebrate them and learn from them. A sense of purpose is something that's often difficult to put into words, but taking the time to figure out and honor your underlying feelings will make all the difference in optimizing how you spend your energy going forward.

Let's take a look at how you can explore your values and use them as a guide for living your best life – living it now and planning for it in the future.

Peter Berry used his values to guide him at a dark moment in his life. He fell into a significant depression when he was first diagnosed with dementia. This is a common and normal reaction to a shocking diagnosis. Berry planned and nearly executed a suicide attempt, but as he contemplated further, he had a flash of inspiration that aligned with how he had lived his life previously. "It was like a light came on, and it seemed to shine across my path showing me the next part of my life as, suddenly, I felt I had a clear mission. Who had been there for me, I thought? No one. What help had Teresa [his wife] and I received? None. That just wasn't right. I didn't want anyone else to go through what I was going through. For the time that I had left – and I had no idea how much time that was going to be – I was going to be the person there for others; I was going

VALUES

to be the person that I wished had been there for me when I got my diagnosis. I was going to be the ordinary bloke in the street who would make sure that no one went through the dark hell of what I had to go through. After all, what I had planned to do was a long-term solution to a short-term problem. I've always been one to problem-solve. So, I got down and took the noose off my neck and I said out loud, "It's Peter Berry 1, Alzheimer's 0."[102]

Performing a Value Inventory

Identifying your core values is an important part of a life review, and sorting through what makes you unique is empowering! Examining your values can be a powerful guiding force when making decisions – it's not always the fastest or most popular choice, but something that will bring alignment with your authentic self. Taking a look back on your life and using your values as your guide can be an eye-opening experience. You have the power to develop a deeper understanding of where you've been and where you're going. By reflecting on moments that highlighted significant aspects of your character, interests, or accomplishments, you can gain tremendous insight into what it is that truly matters to you.

A life review allows us to express gratitude for the chapters we may have looked over multiple times yet never quite appreciated until now. With this newfound focus in hand, we can move ahead with clarity and purpose.

Living your best life means aligning with what you value.

---

[102] Bunt, Deb ; Berry, Peter. Slow Puncture: Living Well With Dementia (p. 32). Kindle Edition.

Peter Berry values self-destiny. He was noticing that he was living in fear of dementia – what it would bring, how it would affect his life, what changes might be coming his way. He would use his biking to assist him in thinking through problems, and on this day, he had another flash of clarity and inspiration. "I got home and decided to draw that monster. I thought if I gave it a face, I would take some of its power away. I was giving it an identity of my own choosing; I was in charge of him and not the other way around. So, I made it the ugliest, most unflattering shape I could. And now that my dementia monster had an identity, I felt I could move on. I had a past, but dementia wanted to take my future, so I had to do all I could to stop the shadows from engulfing my life and my future. This was my future and not one I was prepared to share with an intruder, especially one with such an evil face who had gate-crashed my life without permission."[103]

Berry went even further in his values definition. He named himself a "warrior."

"I would not be defined by my dementia, but I would live alongside it and battle it all of the way. I felt myself drawing my body up, so I stood taller. Suddenly, I had become a general on the battlefield of dementia, a warrior, ready for the fight ahead."[104]

How Do You Accomplish a Life Review?

I have looked at several strategies, and I think that doing the Miller card sort, which I will describe below, works very well.

---

[103] Bunt, Deb ; Berry, Peter. Slow Puncture: Living Well With Dementia (p. 33). Kindle Edition.

[104] Bunt, Deb ; Berry, Peter. Slow Puncture: Living Well With Dementia (pp. 33-34). Kindle Edition.

VALUES

There are several values lists available online, if this doesn't appeal to you. The reason I like the Miller card sort is that it provides an example under each word, so that you spend your time reflecting on the value rather than contemplating what may be meant by that word. It allows for a quicker sort, and I think quick can be helpful as it bypasses some of our resistance to the exercise.

    I highly recommend you print out a PDF of each word to make its own "card." There are 50-100 value cards (depending on the version of the sort you find online) and a few blanks, in the event that a value important to you is not included. You could also just copy each word onto its own note card or sticky note. You will sort all 50-100 cards (extra cards are optional) into one of five categories.

Miller Card Sort Values List

Acceptance To be accepted as I am	**Accuracy** To be accurate in my opinions and beliefs	**Achievement** To have important accomplishments	**Adventure** To have new and exciting experiences
Attractiveness To be physically attractive	**Authority** To be in charge of and responsible for others	**Autonomy** To be self-determined and independent	**Beauty** To appreciate beauty around me

Caring To take care of others	**Challenge** To take on difficult tasks and problems	**Change** To have a life full of change and variety	**Comfort** To have a pleasant and comfortable life
Commitment To make enduring, meaningful commitments	**Compassion** To feel and act on concern for others	**Contribution** To make a lasting contribution in the world	**Cooperation** To work collaboratively with others
Courtesy To be considerate and polite toward others	**Creativity** To have new and original ideas	**Dependability** To be reliable and trustworthy	**Duty** To carry out duties and obligations
Ecology To live in harmony with the environment	**Excitement** To have a life full of thrills and stimulation	**Faithfulness** To be loyal and true in relationships	**Fame** To be known and recognized
Family To have a happy, loving family	**Fitness** To be physically fit and strong	**Flexibility** To adjust to new circumstances easily	**Forgiveness** To be forgiving of others

VALUES

Friendship To have close, supportive friends	**Fun** To play and have fun	**Generosity** To give what I have to others	**Genuineness** To act in a manner that is true to who I am
God's Will To seek and obey the will of God	**Growth** To keep changing and growing	**Health** To be physically well and healthy	**Helpfulness** To be helpful to others
Honesty To be honest and truthful	**Hope** To maintain a positive and optimistic outlook	**Humility** To be modest and unassuming	**Humor** To see the humorous side of myself and the world
Independence To be free from dependence on others	**Industry** To work hard and well at my life tasks	**Inner Peace** To experience personal peace	**Intimacy** To share my innermost experiences with others
Justice To promote fair and equal treatment for all	**Knowledge** To learn and contribute valuable knowledge	**Leisure** To take time to relax and enjoy	**Loved** To be loved by those close to me

Loving To give love to others	**Mastery** To be competent in my everyday activities	**Mindfulness** To live conscious and mindful of the present moment	**Moderation** To avoid excesses and find a middle ground
Monogamy To have one close, loving relationship	**Non-conformity** To question and challenge authority and norms	**Nurturance** To take care of and nurture others	**Openness** To be open to new experiences, ideas, and options
Order To have a life that is well-ordered and organized	**Passion** To have deep feelings about ideas, activities, or people	**Pleasure** To feel good	**Popularity** To be well-liked by many people
Power To have control over others	**Purpose** To have meaning and direction in my life	**Rationality** To be guided by reason and logic	**Realism** To see and act realistically and practically
Responsibility To make and carry out responsible decisions	**Risk** To take risks and chances	**Romance** To have intense, exciting love in my life	**Safety** To be safe and secure

VALUES

Self-Acceptance To accept myself as I am	**Self-control** To be disciplined in my own actions	**Self-esteem** To feel good about myself	**Self-knowledge** To have a deep and honest understanding of myself
Service To be of service to others	**Sexuality** To have an active and satisfying sex life	**Simplicity** To live life simply, with minimal needs	**Solitude** To have time and space where I can be apart from others
Spirituality To grow and mature spiritually	**Stability** To have a life that stays fairly consistent	**Tolerance** To accept and respect those who differ from me	**Tradition** To follow respected patterns of the past
Virtue To live a morally pure and excellent life	**Wealth** To have plenty of money	**World Peace** To work to promote peace in the world	**Other Values:** Create cards as needed for unnamed values

(https://www.motivationalinterviewing.org/sites/default/files/valuescardsort_0.pdf)

    The five categories that the cards can be placed in are: Least important, not very important, neither important nor unimportant, somewhat important, and most important.

Now review each word from the cards and place each in one of the five categories. Each word can go in any **one** of the five categories – it doesn't matter how many cards are already in that pile.

To help you sort the cards, consider the people you admire most and consider your previous experiences.

Once you have the cards sorted, count the number of cards in the most important pile. Are there at least five? If not, review the somewhat important pile and prioritize which card could be moved to the most important pile until you have five cards in the most important pile.

Once you have at least five cards in the most important pile, rank them from the most important to least important to you.

Our goal is to come up with your top five values. Sit with this and take in those five values. Take at least a few minutes if not some protected time for reflection.

The Case for Following Your Values

Personal values are the things that are important to us, the characteristics and behaviors that motivate us and guide our decisions. Believe it or not, writing about your values is an effective psychological intervention. In the short term, writing about personal values makes people feel more powerful, in control, proud, and strong. It also makes them feel more loving, connected, and empathetic toward others. It increases pain tolerance, enhances self-control, and reduces unhelpful rumination after a stressful experience.

While Peter Berry's main core value may have been independence, there was also a value of self-determination, which included deciding that it was acceptable to ask for help, but as you can see, he never lost his desire or value to protect those he loved. "I now need people there with me, taking my hand and pushing the gate open for me. I have always been a proud man, always happy to lead the way, but I now realize that there is nothing wrong with needing help. The hardest thing is to acknowledge it. Teresa [his wife] and Kate [his daughter] were my main support, but sometimes I just didn't want them to know how hard things were. They lived with my dementia every day and I knew they needed the odd break and I still wanted to protect them for as long as I could."[105]

The Five Core Values

Once you know what your values are, it's important to use them as a guiding light during decision times. Then, once you've figured out how to direct your energy in service of these values, you can really maximize the impact of things like medical decision choices, relationships, or personal goals. Take some time to reflect on how these values can inform decisions and shape experiences – going forward, it will empower you to make smart movements that line up with your authentic self!

Most people have at least five values they can identify with. One of my core values is curiosity/learning – discovering new countries, gaining new experiences, enlightening myself about new cultures. Once you have arrived at your list of 5 values, put them in order of priority.

How to Use the Values

Now that you are clear on your values, ask yourself:

---

[105] Bunt, Deb ; Berry, Peter. Slow Puncture: Living Well With Dementia (p. 39). Kindle Edition.

- How would I behave differently?
- How would I work and perform differently?
- What would I start doing?
- What would I stop doing?
- What goals would I set and work towards?
- What difference would this knowledge make in my closest relationships and the people I work with?
- How would I talk to myself and treat myself differently?
- How would I treat others differently?

We're all different, and what makes one person happy may leave another person feeling anxious, hemmed in, or disengaged. Defining your personal values and then living by them can help you to feel more fulfilled and to make choices that make you happy, even if they don't make sense to other people.

What if dementia has taken some of your self-confidence? Peter Berry found some confidence in a research study that he participated in that had him working as a team. "I do believe that being part of a team was a great help to increasing our self-esteem. Rather than being told we [the other research participants who were living with dementia] couldn't do something or that it wasn't worth telling us as we'd only forget, we were actively encouraged to problem-solve and work collaboratively."[106] Could you get your family to be your team? A support group? A dementia cafe? Dementia or memory Cafés are comfortable, social gatherings that allow people experiencing cognitive loss and their family and friends to connect, socialize,

---

[106] Bunt, Deb ; Berry, Peter. Slow Puncture: Living Well With Dementia (p. 110). Kindle Edition.

and build new support networks. You can search for one near you using the Memory Café Directory.[107] Find a place where you can practice making decisions if dementia has you thinking you can't. It is likely you can – with a bit of support.

I would like to tell the story of Mr. P. He used his values to craft what he described as the best medicine.

Mr. P and Sarah's Story

Mr. P had been seeing me for years! The staff knew to give me extra time with him as we ended up chatting and laughing for way too long. Sometimes the nurses or the front-end staff would pop in for the fun – with Mr. P's permission, of course. Mr. P was a tall, thin gentleman with wire-rimmed glasses that didn't hide the twinkle in his eye. His daughter, Sarah, accompanied him to his appointments. A few months back, he had asked Sarah to leave us alone so he could confide a concern to me. When we were alone, he leaned in and said, "I never thought I would say this, but I think I'm losing my wits. I know I've been having trouble coming up with words for quite some time, but I'm 90! About a year ago, I was out for a walk and just didn't know where I was, Dr. Anne – not at all! No clue! I can tell you that scared me. I just sat down on a bus bench and the feeling passed – it kind of lifted. I chalked it up to being tired and took my time getting back home. Since then, I haven't really noticed much else, but the other day, I looked in the mirror and didn't recognize myself! I think you have to test me." We looked for medical issues that might be contributing to these occurrences and did neuropsychological testing. Mr. P had probable Alzheimer's disease. I told Mr. P and Sarah the results of the

---
107 https://www.memorycafedirectory.com

testing. "What now?" I told Mr. P we would start to put a plan together over the next few months. Mr. P accepted occupational therapy to assist with strategies to maintain his independence, allowed Sarah to manage his finances, and gave up driving as he understood his cognitive deficits were affecting his orientation in space, making driving unsafe for him and others. He and I began talking about his legacy and his values, to assist in making decisions for his medical care down the road, as his disease progressed.

"You know, Doc, If I could have anything, it would be to have dinner at my place every week, where everyone was welcome. They would come to tell stories and laugh with me. It is the time with family and friends – I don't care if I don't remember it. It is good enough to be around them for that time. That is the best medicine ever!"

Sarah honored his wishes. She arranged for a simple meal to be catered at Mr. P's house each Sunday evening. Anyone and everyone who had time stopped by. In time, the catering stopped, because a pot-luck meal evolved. Stories and laughter filled the house. Mr. P moved in with Sarah as his dementia progressed, and the meal moved to Sarah's house. He started to remain in a small room away from the crowd as the crowd began to overwhelm him, but individuals would filter in to spend quiet time with him. Sarah just told everyone what he could and could not handle. He transitioned to hospice, and the hospice team joined the Sunday night parties! Mr. P died peacefully at Sarah's home having the best medicine each Sunday night for years and years.

Future Planning

Begin by defining how you'd like to live today. This may be enough for many of you for now. By reflecting on your values and choosing what, if any changes need to occur in your life to align with these values.

Once this is firmly in place and you've practiced living from your values, you may want to do some future planning. We know that dementia will bring changes. And, from Chapter 2, we have faced what some of these changes will be. Armed with this knowledge, with our values to sustain us, we can start to imagine what we would like or how we would imagine what would help us (or those who partner with us) address the question of how we fill our time. What would be some areas for engagement? I asked a few friends (and myself) if they could imagine what may give them joy if they were confined to a wheelchair and only woke from dementia a few hours in a day. What might, from their imagination now, give them a sense of happiness, calm, or joy. Time in nature will be important to me. If I cannot get out into nature due to infirmity, I will request that my children have me near an open window each day where I might feel fresh air and be able to hear birds singing, watch trees swaying, hear wind blowing. I also enjoy watching and hearing the children from the school across the street come out to play, laugh, and squeal at their lunch and recess breaks. A friend of mine says she would value "people watching." She can imagine that she would like to be driven to a town center and just watch people interacting on the street, walking from shop to shop, sitting in cafes. Another friend thought she would like being at a senior center, hearing the activities, seeing people engaged in lectures, activities, and conversations. What do you imagine from this thought experiment?

O'Donohue speaks of imaging hard times ahead and, from his perspective, garner courage to imagine some of those tougher times and therefore plan for them. "A lot of the experiences that we have in the world are torn, broken, hard experiences, and in broken, difficult, lonesome experiences, you can earn a quality of light that is very precious. I often think of it as quarried light. When you come through a phase of pain or isolation or suffering, the light that is given to you at the end of that is a very precious light, and really when you go into something similar again, it is the only kind of light that can mind you. It is the lantern that you will bring you through that pain."[108]

Do a similar thought experiment for housing. When you can no longer drive or transport independently, will your current housing situation still fit you? If yes, what supports would allow for you to get to the activities that will maintain your need for socialization? If not, what may benefit you?

And finally, please extend this thought experiment to functional needs. Instrumental activities of daily living include use of the phone; shopping for groceries; planning, heating, and serving your own meals; managing your medicines; cleaning your house or apartment; getting around on your own, either by car, taxi, or public transportation; managing money and paying bills. Who will you want to assist in these activities and how? Activities of daily living are also activities related to personal care. They include bathing or showering, dressing, getting in and out of bed or a chair, walking, using the toilet, and eating.

---

[108] O'Donohue, John. Walking in Wonder. p. 152.

Please use your thought experiment to decide what you would want for assistance with these activities when the time comes.

I know these can be scary waters to enter. I look to O'Donohue to shore me up when I ask this of you. "Only the imagination has the willingness to witness that which is really complex, dark, paradoxical, contradictory, and awkward within us that which doesn't fit comfortably on the veneer of the social surface. So, we depend on the imagination to troll and retrieve our poignant and wounded complexity which has to remain absent from the social service. The imagination is really the inspired and unconscious Priestess who, against the wishes of all systems and structures, insists on celebrating the liturgy of presence at the banished altars of absence. So, the imagination is faithful to the full home of the heart and all its rooms."[109] This is the value of imagination O'Donohue puts to use in his day-to-day. Imagination is so based in feeling, something that can be fostered and nurtured, even as you live with dementia – taking up a new hobby, searching for meaning in new ways, facing the oncoming disability, and preparing for it.

End-of-Life Choices

I know many of you want to skip this section. And I understand that ... really! But please don't.

Addressing your end-of-life choices is a good idea. And for good reason. We need to make our choices known or the default – aggressive medical care – will be the decision. Death has been a taboo subject, but that is changing. Movements

---
[109] to be added

such as 5 Wishes,[110] Compassion and Choices,[111] and the Conversation Project[112] move discussions forward to understand and deliberate advance directives and articulate choices and wishes for the end of life. Unfortunately, it seems the movement is slow. I had a meeting with 10 individuals, all identified as leaders in aging; only two of us had documented our end-of-life choices and carried on conversations with our families about our wishes.

Articulating end-of-life wishes is possibly the last thing you want to do after a diagnosis of mild cognitive impairment, dementia, Alzheimer's disease, or cognitive decline – this is what I'm told by many patients. "I'm dealing with so much and don't want to consider what lies ahead."

But we know ultimately what lies ahead ... death is inevitable. But how you want to die is a choice. What matters to you? Where do your priorities lie? Two-thirds of American adults haven't completed an advance directive. It's a legal document outlining a person's wishes if they become unable to make their own health care decisions, particularly near the end of life. Make a commitment to record your wishes!

Know that it may not be easy. One-quarter of American adults over age 45 are unwilling to discuss their parents' death with their parents, even if the prognosis is less than six months.[113] Be brave – have the conversation!

---

110 https://www.fivewishes.org/
111 https://www.compassionandchoices.org/
112 https://theconversationproject.org/
113 Lindsay J. Peterson, Debra Dobbs, Hongdao Meng, Alyssa Gamaldo, Kevin O'Neil, and Kathryn Hyer.Sharing End-of-Life Care Preferences with Family Members: Who Has the Discussion and Who Does Not.Journal of Palliative Medicine. Apr 2018.463-472

In a Pew Research Center's Social & Demographic Trends project, adults over 65 years with at least one child, 35 percent of them never spelled out their end-of-life wishes to their children.[114] Try making the important conversation a game – don't leave it to chance. There are two choices that I recommend as tools. One is called Go Wish, a card game about end-of-life preferences developed by Coda Alliance,[115] a community-based, not-for-profit organization helping individuals and families prepare for end-of-life issues. Go Wish is a practical game that has you rank 36 priorities about life and death (e.g., to have family with me; talk about things that scare me; help others; to not be a burden to my family; to remember personal accomplishments). The game asks that family predict what *you* might want – the similarities and differences will spark conversation.

Another option is "Hello" This game was developed by Nick Jehlen of Common Practice.[116]

Hello Has been used in a host of settings (communities, hospitals, hospices), and 75 percent of those who play take some action in either having discussions or completing their advanced directives.[117]

I know "ticking off boxes" is not what you have in mind – it feels too sterile and fixed. But the goal is to have a discussion, so that those who will be assisting you in fulfilling your choices at the end of your life have some guidance. This guidance helps

---

[114] https://www.pewresearch.org/social-trends/2009/08/20/end-of-life-decisions-how-americans-cope/
[115] https://codaalliance.org/
[116] https://commonpractice.com/
[117] Van Scoy, LJ, Reading, JM, Hopkins, M, Smith, B, Dillon, J, Green, MJ, Levi BH. Community Game Day: Using an end-of-life conversation game to encourage advance care planning. Journal of Pain Management Volume 54, Issue 5, November 2017, Pages 680-691.

them tremendously – to assuage guilt, doubts, and regrets. It is truly a great legacy to help them with these choices.

Conclusions

Ultimately, it's up to you to decide what matters most to you and use that as a compass for living your life. This knowledge can then be used as a compass for taking action in your life going forward. A life review can help you gain clarity on how to live more purposefully and make the most of each day. There are so many great tools available for exploring your values that can help guide you towards creating a life that reflects what's important to you – it's up to you to seize the opportunity!

O'Donohue speaks to this creating your life on purpose in a beautiful way. By facing our fears, addressing our life, and living intentionally, we transfigure our lives so that we face a friend rather than a monster in our final days of being on this planet. "Every step of the road of your life you take, your death is beside you. Death often works through the vehicle of fear, so as you begin to transfigure your own fear, you're actually transfiguring the presence of your own death. At the end of your life, when death comes, it won't be some kind of monster forcefully expelling you from the familiar into the unknown, but it can actually be a friend who hides the most truthful image of your own soul. Each day, however, you have to work at transfiguring the fear."[118]

Further, Peter Berry warns that planning must be done, and shelters built for the dementia storm that is ahead. I contend that values are those shelters that Peter speaks of. In the following passage, Peter is describing a day when thinking is foggy or

---
118 O'Donohue, John. Walking in Wonder. p. 83.

befuddled and fear may enter. "I explained that dementia was about those of us living with the condition being forced to build our own shelters from the dementia storm, the storm which you knew was approaching with the passing of each day and the storm which was going to knock you down eventually. We built our own shelters because others did not realise how strong the shelter had to be. And we took refuge in those shelters like wounded animals when the storm clouds gathered, only venturing out when the sun was shining again."[119]

While it's impossible to live life perfectly in alignment with our values 100 percent of the time, knowing what they are is an important first step. Once we're aware of our values, we can make smaller day-to-day choices that align with them – and also use them as a guide when making bigger decisions. Additionally, taking a look back at our lives through the lens of our values can be incredibly helpful in understanding what has been most meaningful to us. And finally, by having this knowledge, we can make more intentional choices going forward about how we want to spend our time. So, take some time to think about your own values – what matters most to you? How do you want to spend your days? And then use that as your compass moving forward.

Peter Berry does! He kept arranging for biking challenges to increase awareness of dementia and to be an example of what strengths can still be seen in those living with dementia. "I was on such a high! Although I did a lot of the planning, which I really enjoyed, I did have some help. I was beginning to learn to accept this and so many people had been involved in the

---

[119] Bunt, Deb ; Berry, Peter. Slow Puncture: Living Well With Dementia (p. 89). Kindle Edition.

planning of the challenge – especially Teresa [his wife] and my old school friend, Norman, who drove the support car – that it gave me a sense of hope. I said before that I didn't want to be defined by my dementia. As I cycled over that week, I realised I was just the old Peter, doing what I did best. And that was a wonderful thing in my life at that moment in time. This made me come to think about my life and I realised that, even though there were some things I could not do, and more things were going to be taken away from me by this dementia, there were still so many things I could achieve. I have always been a glass-half-full person and, as quickly as the dementia monster tried to empty my glass, the best way I could win was to fill it up again. I believe my successful challenge gave my monster a bit of a kick up the backside and he disappeared for a short while, skulking, coming up with a different way he could pin me down."[120]

Points to Remember

- When we focus on our values, we know how we want to live.
- A values inventory can be done with tools such as the Miller card sort and accomplished with a bit of reflecting on moments that highlighted significant aspects of your character, interests, or accomplishments.
- Focusing on core values will provide a guiding light for decisions.

---

[120] Bunt, Deb ; Berry, Peter. Slow Puncture: Living Well With Dementia (pp. 44-45). Kindle Edition.

- End-of-life choices need to be contemplated, acted on (via developing some type of advance care directive), and voiced to those who will implement the plan.

Action Plan

- Gather the resources needed for a values assessment. Would that be a printout of the values from the Miller card sort, someone to scribe for you, or merely a pen, paper, and a quiet corner? Decide what you need to accomplish your values assessment and carve out the time.
- Allow the five core values to be uncovered.
- Take time and energy to ask questions about your life keeping the five core values in mind.
- Repeat these questions for aspects in your life that will need modified plans as you proceed – housing, transportation, personal care.
- Develop some type of advance care directive and articulate your wishes to those who need to hear them. You can do this with a document and discussion or through the playing of a game such as Go Wish or Hello, but move this to an action step, not just a thought experiment.

Resources

Peter Berry and Deb Bunt, *Slow Puncture: Living Well with Dementia*

"This is an inspirational look at both living in the present and coping with dementia." This description from the publisher does a good job summarizing the highlights of this memoir, dictated to a friend Peter meets early in his retirement who accompanies him on bike rides and bike challenges to raise money for dementia awareness. Their friendship introduces Deb to seeing dementia from Peter's point of view and to documenting his ups and downs, acceptance of the disease, and joy in his every day.

John O'Donohue and John Quinn, *Walking in Wonder: Eternal Wisdom for a Modern World*

"These timeless exchanges, collated and introduced by Quinn, span a number of years and explore themes such as imagination, landscape, the medieval mystic Meister Eckhart, aging, and death." This description by the publisher reveals the similarities with Slow Puncture. These are the experts on life, thoughtfully collated by a friend, for one who no longer can speak (O'Donohue died in 2017). Both O'Donohue and Berry speak lyrically and have insights on life and living worth reading.

Chapter 8

PLANNING AND PREPARING FOR EMOTIONAL AND PHYSICAL CHANGES, ADAPTATIONS, AND LIMITS

Overview

Although about 70 percent of Americans prefer to die at home and avoid hospitalization or intensive care during the terminal phase of illness, recent data show that only around 60 percent actually die at home or in hospice care.[121] There are some opinions on why this continues to occur, including the bias in western culture that all illness can be cured, the training of healthcare professionals focused on cure rather than quality of life, pharmaceutical focus in the treatment of disease, and people willing to undergo unwanted treatment for the sake of their loved ones

---

[121] Pollock K, Is home always the best and preferred place of death? BMJ 2015; 351:h4855.)

(rather than having open and honest conversations). Further, as humans we often don't make rational decisions, especially about end of life, since we don't have much time to experience or practice these types of decisions. Finally, again as humans, we often go with the status quo, which is usually prolonging life, not shifting to a focus on quality of life. It is difficult to die in peace because our healthcare system is deeply ingrained with a culture of continuing treatment, and we may not fully realize the extent of this influence.[122]

Tom DeBaggio, whom you met in Chapter 6, an individual living with dementia and author of *When It Gets Dark: An Enlightened Reflection on Life with Alzheimer's*, shows the struggle of facing death and the confusion it can bring. "Most people don't take time to think about death. When death shows its head, it is impossible to put aside thoughts about the shortness of life and how little is accomplished while we live out our meager time. With Alzheimer's there is plenty of time to ponder death, too much really. It makes me want to be run over by a fancy car. Anguished days of confusion and unreadable secrets puff up time and bring sudden yelps and rainbows behind my eyes where the tears live."[123]

How do we then prepare when the healthcare system and our humanness stack preparing against us? How can we safely go into the waters of facing our death so that we may find the death that we want. You've done much of the hard work in the preceding chapters. You've looked at your values. You've contemplated what matters most to you. You've grounded yourself

---

[122] Gijsbertsen B, Kremer JAM. We all want to die in peace - So why don't we? BMJ Support Palliat Care. 2021 Sep;11(3):318-321

[123] DeBaggio, Thomas. When It Gets Dark: An Enlightened Reflection on Life with Alzheimer's (p. 114). Free Press. Kindle Edition

in purpose. Now it is time to gently go the extra few courageous miles and imagine how you want the end to be. You must face that there will be an end – not an easy task and one that does not always get support from family or friends. Those who say, "No – don't talk like that. That isn't happening, you are not dying."

But we know that it does happen. Since we often don't speak of it, it happens in darkness. Let's bring it into the light. Let's talk about what it looks like so that it is more familiar and easier to handle, so that it becomes familiar. I would love to do this through the lens of palliative care.

Palliative Approach to Quality of Life in Care

"Palliative" is a term used in the medical field and beyond to describe care approaches that focus on improving the quality of life for patients with a life-threatening illness and their families. It aims to relieve suffering by identifying, assessing, and treating pain and other physical, psychosocial, and spiritual problems. Palliative care can be provided whether an illness is potentially curable, chronic, or life-threatening; is appropriate for patients with noncancer diagnoses; and can be administered in conjunction with curative-aimed therapies at any stage of the illness. The philosophy of palliative care addresses the entire person and their family in a holistic way, dealing with values, emotions, connections, grief, spirituality/existentialism/meaning, creativity, and legacy in addition to the person's physical/disease-related needs (which are typically the major focus of a medical approach).

Though the positives of palliative care are evident, very little has been done to adopt a palliative approach to care for persons living with dementia. Sadly, few studies have been done addressing palliative interventions in advanced dementia, and most don't address important considerations such as quality of life, antipsychotic use, analgesic use, and decisional conflict in care partners.

One of the studies highlighted the difficulties for families in discussing or engaging in planning conversations on palliative care for a person with dementia.[124] These conversations were hindered by knowledge deficiencies and differences, a lack of understanding of the disease trajectory of dementia, the unpredictable nature of dementia itself, and religious and socioeconomic issues. Many of the chapters of this book attempt to remedy these obstacles.

Emotions and Hope, Especially Around Initial Diagnosis

Interventions to cultivate hope improve quality of life and reduce symptoms of depression in populations with neurological disorders.[125] So many people with dementia have a period of psychological distress in the period after diagnosis. For those who are given support (and hope), this distress markedly decreases from occurring in 30 percent of people to 5 percent of people while for those left without support, the psychological distress

---

[124] Hines S, McCrow J, Abbey J, Foottit J, Wilson J, Franklin S, Beattie E. The effectiveness and appropriateness of a palliative approach to care for people with advanced dementia: a systematic review. JBI Libr Syst Rev. 2011;9(26):960-1131. doi: 10.11124/01938924-201109260-00001. PMID: 27820410.careHines, 2011

[125] Lai ST, Lim KS, Low WY, Tang V. Positive psychological interventions for neurological disorders: A systematic review. Clin Neuropsychol. 2019 Apr;33(3):490-518. doi: 10.1080/13854046.2018.1489562. Epub 2018 Jun 24. PMID: 29938575.Lai, 2019).

increases from 30 to 45 percent of people in the unsupported group of the study.[126]

The goal of this book is to provide support and hope. The goal is to understand that cognitive loss is a chronic condition and that by defining your values, your dreams and your purpose, you are building your hope and your resilience. And by addressing the elephant in the room, that this is also a terminal disease, you are creating agency and mastery over the full course of this disease.

Planning

An early diagnosis is ideal in that it opens the door to active participation in determining future care and treatment. It helps people to plan while they are still able to make important decisions on their care and support needs and on financial and legal matters. It also helps them and their families to receive practical information, advice, and guidance as they face new challenges together. Family members supporting someone further progressed in their dementia will also benefit from the education, but making decisions together is most ideal. Care partners report their biggest challenge in caregiving is uncertainty about the suffering of their family member or friend.

One of the few studies that included individuals with dementia and their families found five themes around end-of-life choices: Individuals and families wished to avoid dehumanizing treatment and care; they wanted support in confronting

---

[126] Mazurek J, Szcześniak D, Lion KM, Dröes RM, Karczewski M, Rymaszewska J. Does the Meeting Centres Support Programme reduce unmet care needs of community-dwelling older people with dementia? A controlled, 6-month follow-up Polish study. Clin Interv Aging. 2019 Jan 11;14:113-122. doi: 10.2147/CIA.S185683. PMID: 30666097; PMCID: PMC6331064.Mazurek, 2019

emotionally difficult conversations; they needed assistance in navigating existential tension; they needed guidance in defining personal autonomy; and finally, they wanted direction in the face of their lack of confidence in the healthcare system. When PLWD and their families prepare well, they often get to a place of appreciation, as Wendy Mitchell, a person living with early-onset dementia and author of Somebody I Used to Know, has. "Dementia won't steal everything, even though it can feel that way now. Even though forgetting my daughters is my worst fear, nature will ensure that the tides rise, the sun sets, the brooks keep on babbling. I am heartened to understand that dementia is nothing more than a trick of my mind, and I can outwit it if I stare at my photographs hard enough, if I find the whirlpool that is still there – the tiny gem to be appreciated in all this."[127]

Understanding and exploring the five themes will help begin to guide the end-of-life planning angst. We will address many of these themes in this chapter and the next two chapters about medical/legal issues and communicating with family and healthcare providers. Hang in there. We will be going deep, but the preparation will make living easier and calmer.

Avoid Dehumanizing Treatment and Care

Medical Issues and What can be Modified as Disease Transitions.

Another author you will meet in this chapter is Katy Butler, who wrote The Art of Dying Well: A Practical Guide to a Good End of Life. She wrote this brave book because she watched

---

[127] Mitchell, Wendy. Somebody I Used to Know (p. 62). Random House Publishing Group. Kindle Edition

what happened to her and her mother as her father became ill and the medical system controlled their lives and made their decisions for them. She writes, "We were ignorant of medicine's limits, and the harm it can do, when it approaches an aging human being in the same way as it does the bodies of the young. Two years later, my father was given a pacemaker to correct his slow heartbeat. This tiny electronic device made him, as he put it, 'live too long' by forcing his heart to outlive his brain."[128]

Another personal anecdote within Katy Butler's book tells of when a brother is accusing his sister of hastening their other brother's death with morphine, and the hospice nurse calmly and gently corrects him and says, "Your brother is dying, and this is what dying looks like."[129]

Here, I would like to tell you what a typical dementia end-stage looks like so that you can decide when to shift from medical to supportive care only. I know that line is different for everyone. I know that family members wonder and struggle and debate, but if you can help them by being as clear as you can now, they will have an easier time making those decisions for you, and you will leave a legacy that is priceless – you will leave them without doubt and regret so that they can grieve and hold the fondest memories. You will also leave behind an example of the incredible courage that is often lacking in our death-resistant society. You will leave the legacy of facing something difficult or taboo and shatter the control that the taboo can hold over

---

[128] Butler, Katy. The Art of Dying Well: A Practical Guide to a Good End of Life (p. 2). Scribner. Kindle Edition.
[129] Butler, Katy. The Art of Dying Well: A Practical Guide to a Good End of Life (p. 2). Scribner. Kindle Edition.

us. In doing this, you will change the world in a positive way for those left behind.

Wendy Mitchell discusses making these decisions with her daughters and admits that it was difficult. "Today Gemma and Sarah are on their way round to help me write my lasting power of attorney document – in effect, what my wishes are when I'm no longer able to articulate them. I think of some of the questions that I've already written in pencil, and fight that feeling inside that so desperately wants to protect my girls from having to do this."[130]

When during the discussion, one daughter is reluctant to speak, her other daughter gains the courage to speak up. "'But if Mum had already lost capacity and we were making those decisions for her, she wouldn't want to survive and continue to deteriorate with dementia in control,' Gemma says gently. 'She wouldn't want to get better and live in the dementia world.'

"I smile, feeling the breath I've been holding onto leave me."

"'Good job we're talking now, otherwise you'd be falling out and arguing over decisions when I couldn't help put things right,' I say with a smile, trying in some way to brighten the mood."[131]

This was a courageous family showing us the way to move forward in these talks and these discussions.

---

130 Mitchell, Wendy. Somebody I Used to Know (p. 57). Random House Publishing Group. Kindle Edition.
131 Mitchell, Wendy. Somebody I Used to Know (p. 58). Random House Publishing Group. Kindle Edition.

Usual Course of Late-Stage Dementia

Eating/Swallowing

Feeding problems often herald the final stage of dementia. The difficulty with eating may begin in the moderate stages of dementia. An individual may no longer be able to coordinate the act of bringing food to their mouth or develop issues with "pocketing food in their cheeks", meaning that they can no longer coordinate moving food from the front of their mouth to the back of their mouth in order to initiate swallowing. Other indications of impaired swallowing include coughing and choking, or a hoarse voice as fluids remain on the vocal cords. Finally, people with dementia begin to slow or minimize their eating and begin to resist or refuse to eat. All of these things are natural and expected. Unfortunately, we often combat the decreased drive to eat with protein shakes or extended dining sessions lasting over an hour. In our medical framework, we focus on the nutritional aspects of eating: are adequate calories being consumed? To feed someone when their body is rejecting the process can bring on several complications. The body knows how to slow down and begin to accept the dying process. When we fight this, people are more likely to suffer from congestion in their lungs or distress in their stomach. Food has so many meanings. It is the fuel our body needs to function, but we have a more personal, often spiritual, connection to food. In times of both sickness and celebration, we gather around food. But when a disease has progressed to end stages, loss of appetite and weight loss are a normal part of preparing for death, and it is perfectly fine to allow this to occur without medical intervention.

Dehydration

Dehydration is also normal as someone nears the end of their life with dementia. Dehydration allows the body to comfortably shut down without excess secretions, sweating, urination, and defecation. This is a time for family to learn to be with you in another personal spiritual way rather than focusing on food or hydration.

Infections

Infections are common in the late stage of dementia, as they may have been in the moderate stages. The infections usually occur in the urinary tract or the lungs (pneumonia). There are a host of reasons that any individual living with dementia would become susceptible to infections in the late stage of their disease. Often the immune system is impaired due to age and diminished nutrition. As mentioned above, due to dementia, the ability to cough to clear the airway is impaired, and urine flow is decreased, limiting the ability to clear bacteria from the urinary tract. Treating these infections with antibiotics becomes futile as the underlying cause will not change. In addition, the antibiotics themselves are not without side effects. Studies in adults with advanced dementia reveal that those who receive antibiotics have a diminished quality of life compared to those who do not receive antibiotics.[132] The goal can shift to providing symptom control rather than trying to treat the infection, and the quality of life improves.

---

[132] Mitchell SL. CLINICAL PRACTICE. Advanced Dementia. N Engl J Med. 2015 Jun 25;372(26):2533-40. doi: 10.1056/NEJMcp1412652. PMID: 26107053; PMCID: PMC4539157

Hospitalizations

Finally, individuals are sent to the hospital in the late stage of dementia for a number of reasons, but the two most common are dehydration and sleepiness (change in mental status, difficulty arousing the individual). Hospitalization in late-stage dementia is often more harmful than helpful. Hospitalizations are rife with burdensome and costly testing and interventions, and individuals with dementia are twice as likely to be hospitalized than those without dementia.[133] Hospital settings are a major risk to those with advanced dementia; delirium nearly always develops, resulting in either physical or medical restraints that may in turn result in bed sores, aspiration, psychological stress, and, potentially, death. Caregiver burden, psychological stress, and an increase in depression are reported with the decision for hospitalization. I have also witnessed family caregivers experience the trauma of an acute hospitalization that results in distrust of the healthcare system as delirium develops and medical advice from medical specialists is variable.

"But I can't withhold hospital care!" is what I hear from many families. Let's step back and imagine how many of these "medical emergencies" can be handled in the home or residence (e.g., assisted living, continuing care community, skilled nursing facility) rather than the hospital. Reimagine the late stage of dementia being attended to in the home/residential setting, with the focus shifting from medical intervention to comfort. The change in mental status due to an infection is addressed with cold ice chips during times of wakefulness, medication for fever and/or pain, and the ability to sleep either to recovery (most

---
[133] Alzheimer Association Fact and Figures, 2023

common) or death. This scene is peaceful and expected. Where do the difficulties lie? Family may be on a roller coaster of ups and downs, wondering if this is the time my family member will die. But it can be a time of reflection, appreciation, and spiritual growth. Imagine instead that we call in counselors (social or spiritual) and conduct reflective readings while families sit at the bedside. That approach shifts away from running to the hospital, and sitting at the bedside when there are tubes of dripping liquid, buzzers, and beepers. There are other ways. I sat at my mother's bedside on several occasions in her last two years of life. I sat quietly speaking with her (and prayed she heard me), sometimes making amends for being a judging and resistive daughter, sometimes laughing about good times. I also visited with friends and family who came to sit with me, to sit with us. At times, I worked – writing grants, papers, and clinical notes. At times, I just gazed out the window at the bird feeder and the gathering of birds. Some days it was difficult emotionally, but mostly it was peaceful. My mother recovered from countless urinary tract infections and two or three bouts of pneumonia before she eventually closed her mouth to further food. This is the usual way.

Terminal Agitation

At times, what is known as terminal agitation occurs. This may occur in those with or without dementia. Hopefully, you have hospice involved and they can recommend treatment to assist with this. Medications such as pain relievers and anxiety medications may be helpful – medications that are often avoided during our time of living with dementia but become needed and necessary at the end of life.

Support in Confronting Emotionally Difficult Conversations

If you avoid or postpone a tough conversation, it can damage your relationships and have other negative consequences. While it may feel uncomfortable, especially if you dislike conflict, you can develop skills to tackle these difficult talks by changing your mindset. These ideas can be used by you AND your family members.

And, like Wendy Mitchell, many do not want to have to put their family members through the difficult conversations, but with courage, they know they must.

Some tips that can make having a difficult conversation easier are sprinkled throughout this book. Here are a few direct suggestions.

Approach the Situation with a Curious and Respectful Mindset

People who tend to avoid conflict often prioritize being liked. However, being liked is not always the most important factor. One can try to approach the conversation with an open mind and a sincere interest in learning. Approach the conversation with a curious and respectful attitude toward both yourself and the other person. This will often lead to mutual respect and vulnerability. Even if the topic is challenging, the dialogue can still be supportive as long as both parties show respect for each other's perspectives. Remember to expect the same level of respect for your own viewpoints.

Concentrate on Listening, Rather Than Speaking

During a difficult conversation, it is more important to listen, reflect, and observe than to talk excessively. When you pay close attention and remain neutral, it helps others open up. To show that you understand what they're saying, repeat back their statements. You may paraphrase what the other person said: "What I hear you saying is X, is that right?" This technique is referred to as reflective listening.

Be Direct

To resolve uncomfortable situations, confront the issue directly. Engage in a polite and honest conversation with the other person to discuss the problem in detail. Speaking truthfully and respectfully fosters positive relationships, even in challenging conversations.

Do Not Delay the Conversation

How often is your response something like, "I don't want to talk about it" or "I'll bring it up soon"? Deal with the conversation right away instead of postponing it for a more convenient time in the future.

Anticipate a Favorable Result

When having a conversation, think about the long-term benefits for your relationship. By focusing on positive outcomes and advantages, your mindset and self-talk will become more positive and productive.

Navigate Existential Tension

What is existential tension or anxiety? Existential tension or anxiety is a feeling of dread or panic that arises when a person confronts the limitations of their existence. Thoughts of death, the meaningless of life, or the insignificance of self, can all trigger existential tension or anxiety. A diagnosis such as dementia is likely to trigger existential anxiety.

This existential anxiety is part of life. Unfortunately, we all go through it at some time. It is especially present when you are reminded of changes in your cognition on a daily basis.

Wendy Mitchell is dealing with the losses and the grief as she loses some of her function. She doesn't dwell on it, but it is part of her new day-to-day life, and reminds her that she needs to continually adapt and navigate her personal existential tension. In the following quote, she is discussing the loss of her ability to follow a recipe. "But more than anything, a real, visceral grief at saying another goodbye, this time to baking, something I've done my whole life. From baking the first fairy cakes as a child to teaching my girls how to do the same, it's always been there, a constant. There wasn't a gloomy day that a bit of baking couldn't cheer."[134]

Because it's an inherent part of being human, existential tension is not something that will permanently disappear. Coping with existential anxiety is a process not of overcoming it, but of learning to live well despite feelings of existential anxiety. Coping strategies that can assist with existential anxiety include accepting the uncertainty. Sometimes there are no clear-cut answers in life, so it can be helpful to accept and

---

[134] Mitchell, Wendy. Somebody I Used to Know (p. 55). Random House Publishing Group. Kindle Edition.

even appreciate the ambiguity and uncertainty. Letting go of the need to control everything can be a freeing experience.

Watch your thoughts for patterns. Can you think of moments when you feel less anxious and more energized? What usually causes this feeling, and how can you incorporate more of these experiences into your life?

Instead of avoiding your anxiety because it feels overwhelming, face it head-on by taking small steps. Begin by listing all of the major issues causing you stress. Select the one that is currently causing you the most trouble and divide it into smaller parts. From there, you can establish achievable goals and create actionable steps to address each one.

We have spoken about mindfulness, gratitude, and using a therapist or spiritual counselor as well to deal with grief, stress, and the difficulty of dealing with the diagnosis of dementia. Utilize the strategies that have helped you in the past or adopt new strategies for this new situation.

Can you sit with a cup of tea and imagine what may help ground you? What would allow the feeling of panic to lift? I have a meditation practice that began as I needed a way to ground myself during my mother's illness, changes, and ultimate death from dementia. When I become panicked or overwhelmed by some situation, I know to sit in meditation, and this regulates my emotions and brings me back to a place where I can think and function.

Many of the authors you've met use exercise. Peter Berry always feels better after a ride. Tom DeBaggio found all writing and clarity after a walk. Tom also found calm by working in his garden. What could have that clarifying or calming effect on you? Begin to plan for it.

This is part of why you've been exploring sights, sounds, smells, and sensations. Wendy Mitchell speaks of crawling into bed and covering her head with the duvet. For me, it would be tucking into the couch – the corner of the couch acts as a hug for me, tucking me in. One of my children, now in their mid-20s, still loves the sensation of one of their blankets – soft, sensual, and light, not too heavy.

Here are some words of Wendy Mitchell as she faced her existential anxiety. Wendy begins her story with how she discovered she was dealing with dementia and where she looked for answers. At first, like many, she was discouraged by her diagnosis, but then she found Keith Oliver, a gentleman living with dementia, an author, and an advocate. "His story was so positive: he talked about how he felt that his health had maintained a good level since his diagnosis thanks to his determination to live life to the full and focus on the things he enjoyed. By the time the eight-minute clip [she was watching a video of Mr. Oliver speaking] has come to an end, life really doesn't seem as bleak. The ideas I had about what a person with dementia looks and sounds like have been challenged. Keith looks so normal, and I must look no different; he still does the things he enjoys, and so I could, too. It's not so much mortality that hits me full on, but that sense of time – or, rather, lack of it. That's what dementia steals, the future you imagine all laid out in front of you, with no idea when something more final might come."[135]

---

[135] Mitchell, Wendy. Somebody I Used to Know (p. 41). Random House Publishing Group. Kindle Edition

Defining Personal Autonomy

In its simplest sense, autonomy is about a person's ability to act on his or her own values and interests. What can be found in many of the first-person narratives that you have read about in this book is that "fog", confusion, anger, frustration, or vacancy may cloud your days. Several authors describe it well. You can see it in the anger of Greg O'Brien in *On Pluto*, Thomas DeBaggio in *When It Gets Dark: An Enlightened Reflection on Life with Alzheimer's*, and Wendy Mitchell in *Someone I Used to Know*. Most describe redefining their autonomy and preparing for its loss.

Wendy Mitchell's words were chosen for this chapter because of how she prepared for the times of vacancy and the accompanying panic that would begin to overtake her. She heeded the words of a neurologist to prepare for these periods – to breathe in and out and remain calm and know that they would pass. She then set up a memory room, with pictures of her fondest memories strung on the wall with clips on a wire. She describes several times when the confusion would begin to flood her mind, and she would find a safe spot to sit, have a cup of tea, and wait for the feeling to lift. She would breathe and take in the sights, usually focusing away from crowds and toward nature.

Ms. Mitchell, and others, also claim their autonomy by finding purpose. Wendy Mitchell speaks of becoming the "cake lady" to a senior center as a way to find purpose soon after she retired. It helped ground her as she worked out how she wanted to spend her time. She found that space safe for the symptoms she was having at the time, mostly word-finding difficulty. "Word abandons me mid-conversation, or if I forget someone's name from one week to the next. They don't know the old Wendy; they aren't watching me as closely as those who have worked with me for years, who are perplexed by the difference. I can relax there. I don't have to be on guard, disguising any slip-ups; these people are just grateful for my sweet offerings. I am known as the cake lady, a new identity I've carved from sugar and flour but one that suits me so much better than anything the doctors had written in my notes."[136]

And finally, we will look to Ms. Mitchell for how she adapts her definition. She talks of "losing" books but finding poetry. "I've found myself rediscovering the delights of poems, of books that I used to read to the girls when they were tiny. There are the losses, but there are also the gains, and for another fleeting moment I realize that a progressive illness can focus the mind in a very special way."[137]

Addressing Lack of Confidence in the Healthcare System

Also peppered throughout the first-person narratives and medical literature is the sense of distrust and a lack of confidence in clinical information and support available to people living with dementia from the health care setting. And, because of this, many are reluctant to specify their advanced care plans, talk about the end-of-the-disease trajectory, and face the inevitable cognitive deterioration, and they feel locked into a predefined pathway for care.

---

136 Mitchell, Wendy. Somebody I Used to Know (p. 52). Random House Publishing Group. Kindle Edition.

137 Mitchell, Wendy. Somebody I Used to Know (p. 95). Random House Publishing Group. Kindle Edition.

Even when people do complete an advance care plan, they or family often feel unprepared for the decisions that may occur downstream, such as limiting treatment of chronic diseases so that the time spent in end-stage dementia may be shortened.

Many health care advocates are uncertain how much leeway they have in interpreting the advance care plan preferences. They are especially leery about conditions that they believe may be treatable in the face of this terminal disease. This is likely due to the society-based norms around doing everything, rather than tempering care, and their training within this society.

Finally, the ability to achieve person-centered care in an institutional setting seems troublesome to many. As this can be so troublesome to many, Wendy Mitchell wanted her daughters to know she prefers institutional care to having care done by her daughters – a theme I've heard from many individuals. And it's important to let your family know what your preference is and when there is flexibility in that preference.

"'I'm sure we've spoken of this before, but this is what I've written in pencil: If I no longer have the mental capacity to choose my place of residence or become unsafe at home, my attorneys have my approval to choose a suitable residential home. …' I pause. Both of them are looking at their laps. 'I never want you to be my carers. You're my daughters and always will be.' 'Yes, we know, Mum,' Sarah says softly. 'If you're sure …'"[138]

There are many family members who cannot handle the physical care when care needs become too much, and the only affordable alternative is a long-term care institution. At times,

---

138 Mitchell, Wendy. Somebody I Used to Know (p. 59). Random House Publishing Group. Kindle Edition.

it is this difficult conversation that I am asked to have with a family who did not clarify wishes with the individual living with dementia—assuring them that their family member would not want extreme sacrifice in the face of advancing dementia, but that emotional support while others provide some of the physical care is preferred. Be sure to think this through and inform your family what your wishes are.

Openly Talking About Death, Planning, Exploring All Options

What is a good death for you? In this section, we will be discussing some of the options that don't always come up, but that many people with dementia ask me about. Some think this topic is difficult to consider, but usually not the person living with dementia. They often want to know their choices – all of their choices. They don't need to choose whatever is presented, but they do want to know the choices exist.

Almost every first-person narrative I've read has spoken about contemplating assisted death. We know that most people with dementia think about it – the idea that you are faced with a terminal illness that will ultimately cause you to lose capacity and agency is what people describe as the most frightening aspect of the disease. Physician-assisted death is legal in 10 U.S. states and the District of Columbia. It is an option given to individuals by law in Colorado, the District of Columbia, Hawaii, Maine, New Jersey, New Mexico, Oregon, Vermont, and Washington. It is an option given to individuals via court decision in Montana and California. The caveat is that one must have a terminal diagnosis, have capacity to make the decision, and have only six months to live. Therefore, physician-assisted death is not an option for individuals living with dementia in the U.S., as by the time the prognosis is six months, capacity to make the decision has been lost.

Dignitas[139] is a Swiss not-for-profit member-based society that advocates, educates, and supports for improving care and choice in life and at life's end. People from anywhere in the world can join, but to participate in an assisted death, an individual would need to go to Switzerland. The society uses an advisory concept of combining palliative care, suicide-attempt prevention, advance directives, and assisted dying as the basis for decision-making to shape life until the end. According to Swiss law, as long as a person has capacity, they may choose to die as long as it is not for "motivated for selfish reasons." The process is well researched and available. The story of some individuals with dementia who have chosen to use Dignitas was told in a 2011 television documentary entitled *Choosing to Die* presented by Terry Pratchett. Mr. Pratchett was an acclaimed author of more than 30 books, including the *Discworld* series, and an individual living with dementia who was contemplating assisted death. *Choosing to Die* follows the journey of Peter Smedley, a 71-year-old man with motor neuron disease, dying by assisted death at Dignitas. A recent book entitled *In Love: A Memoir of Love and Loss* by Amy Bloom also describes the process as she accompanies (somewhat unwillingly and reluctantly) her husband, who had been diagnosed with Alzheimer's dementia, in his choice to use Dignitas for his assisted death. The Hasting Center[140] has an interview with Ms. Bloom on its website.

---

139 http://www.dignitas.ch/
140 https://www.thehastingscenter.org/

Many would like something similar in other countries, as they do not want to have to travel or have their families travel through this process away from home and support. Wendy Mitchell is vehement about it in her writings. She describes a discussion in one of her support groups. The woman she is quoting in the beginning of the excerpt is someone in her support group. "Well, I've already booked my place at Dignitas," she says. "When I can't take care of myself anymore, I'm not going to put myself into the hands of a care home that can't look after me properly, so when the time comes, I'll go to the euthanasia clinic in Switzerland and end my own life." The rest of the room falls silent. I find myself nodding in agreement, but then glance at Sarah [Wendy's daughter] from the corner of my eye; her head is down. Guilt stings inside at the thought she caught me nodding, but I can't deny that this has been the most empowering statement I've heard all day. With any progressive illness it's the lack of control that's the hardest thing to live with. For me, if I can find a way of living with dementia, shouldn't I be allowed to find a way of dying with it too? It's not a conversation I thought I'd be having in my head today. This morning the conversation between us six women focused on what we could do, but this afternoon it feels like decisions are taken out of our hands – unless we claim them back like the woman who insists she's going to Dignitas. I admire her for already making that decision, particularly as I shuffle out of the room feeling so despondent, frustrated, detached and in despair. ... But with regards to me, that was something I'd never considered. I admired that woman's conviction, her determination to end her life in Switzerland, her way. But I could never do that. I could never ask my girls to travel with me because just the thought of them traveling back alone is enough to break my heart. And so, it's the illegality of euthanasia that I find so frustrating, the fact that another decision has been taken out of my hands – this time by the laws of the land. It's when I think like this, when I don't feel like I have control, or rights, that I start feeling panicky inside. When all the what-ifs or whatabout-whens come rushing up from my gut and squeeze the words right out of my mouth; when the tears prick the back of my eyes, when I feel scared. What will happen to me when I go over the edge into that person I don't know? Will I be blissfully unaware? Will I not even recognize the pain written across the two faces that mean the most to me – Sarah and Gemma [Wendy's daughters]? Euthanasia would save us all from that."[141]

In the United States, the Final Exit[142] pushes for legalization of assisted death with less restrictions. Death with Dignity[143] and Compassion and Choices[144] are two other organizations that advocate for people exploring their own choices for end-of-life conditions. These movements are expanding the conversation. The following is excerpted from a Death with Dignity website page that features commonly asked questions about physician-assisted death.[145]

What is Death with Dignity Legislation?

Death with dignity, or medical aid-in-dying, statutes allow certain adults with terminal illness to request and obtain a prescription for medication to end their lives in a peaceful manner.

---

141 Mitchell, Wendy. Somebody I Used to Know (p. 104). Random House Publishing Group. Kindle Edition.
142 https://finalexitnetwork.org/
143 https://deathwithdignity.org/
144 https://www.compassionandchoices.org/resource/history-end-life-choice-movement
145 https://deathwithdignity.org/resources/faqs/

The acts outline the process of obtaining such medication, including safeguards to protect both patients and physicians.

In states where physician-assisted dying is legal, there is no state program for participation in the existing aid-in-dying laws and people do not apply to state health departments. It is up to eligible patients and licensed physicians to implement the act on an individual, case-by-case basis.

Can My Family Member or a Proxy Request Participation in Medical Aid in Dying on My Behalf (For Example, If I Am in a Coma or Suffer From Alzheimer's Disease or Dementia?

No. The law requires that you ask to participate voluntarily on your own behalf and meet all the eligibility criteria at the time of your request.

Can Physician-Assisted Death Laws be Used with Advanced Directives?

No. Advance directives are documents that describe what you as a dying person want done (or not done) medically if you can no longer make decisions for yourself. Aid-in-dying laws cannot be used under advance directives for this reason."

What Can Be Done in the US, if You Would Like to Limit Your Time in the Late Stage of Dementia?

You are allowed to decline any medical interventions and you may stop eating and drinking. You may make these wishes known to your health advocates, but they must be willing to agree with you and continue on this course.

I know of a podcaster whose mother told her that she didn't want life-saving treatment, nor did she want to eat when she entered the stage of dementia when she could no longer feed herself. The podcaster said that her mother "changed" and was a different person when she was in her later stages of dementia, and this new person wanted to live.

Feelings regarding eating are difficult. There are so many layers to our beliefs about food – it is nourishment, but it is also a symbol of love. If your family member believes they are withholding love, they will not do it! You must educate them about this difference if you want them to make that decision for you. Ask for love in new ways if you do not want them to feed you! Ask for time spent massaging lotion into your hands while they take the same time, they would to feed you, or ask them to read you a story or sing a few songs with you. Give them alternative actions – so that they can fill you with love rather than filling you with food.

Guide your family on what you would like them to do if it appears you've changed your mind and want to eat; as the podcaster's mother appeared to change. Let your family know how much flexibility you'd be comfortable with if this scenario should arise. For example, I've told my children that I would like them to honor my request to stop eating, I have told them that hospice can be called in to help them with implementing this choice of mine and to offer emotional support to them around this decision. Realize that implementing the choice to ask that feedings stop for someone else may be too difficult for some people. Most of us will be happy if our children or family do their best in making a decision with the information they have present. If it seems a family member has changed, as it did for the podcaster, honor the voice of the person using their voice that day.

There is a time when feeding becomes more problematic than helpful. I just spoke to a friend who sat at her father-in-law's bedside as he passed. Her brother-in-law fed his father each time he opened his eyes, which caused stomach discomfort, coughing, and a need for more medications. My friend tried to educate her brother-in-law that the food was causing the distress, but her brother-in-law wanted to show love (and her father-in-law wanted to accept so that his son could show love). We don't often sit at bedsides, so we have lost the art of sitting, singing, praying, reading, whispering, mummering, cooing, stroking, and just sending love. Tell your family that not feeding can be a better way, but that love can still be expressed in those other ways.

Katy Butler, in *The Art of Dying Well*, has crafted a letter to help guide her family and healthcare providers on her wishes. It is explicit and complete regarding her wishes to avoid being fed or placed on intravenous fluids, testing, or thickening of liquids. There are also specific advance directives, but I think a letter such as this is a wonderful addition to anything that discusses your advance directives.

It is crucial that you have someone to advocate for these wishes. That someone is not always your closest family member, who is torn by their desire to prolong your time on this planet even if you've stated that is not your wish.

Why a shift to focus on comfort or slow medicine is likely beneficial with advancing illness.

Katy Butler puts it very well in her introductory comments in *The Art of Dying Well*. "In the years I've spent listening to hundreds of people's stories of good and difficult declines and deaths, I've learned one thing: people who are willing to contemplate their aging, vulnerability, and mortality often live better lives in old age and illness, and experience better deaths, than those who don't. They keep shaping lives of comfort, joy, and meaning, even as their bodies decline. They get clear-eyed about the trajectory of their illnesses, so they can plan. They regard their doctors as their consultants, not their bosses. They seek out medical allies who help them thrive, even in the face of disappointment and adversity, and they prepare for a good death. They enroll in hospice earlier, and often feel and function better – and sometimes even live longer – than those who pursue maximum treatment. They make peace with the coming of death, and seize the time to forgive, to apologize, and to thank those they love. They rethink the meaning of "hope." And they often die with less physical suffering, and just as much attention to the sacred, as our ancestors did."[146]

Points to Remember

- To avoid having decisions made for you, you must face the discomfort of looking into the future and plan. Those that plan are less likely to receive unnecessary medical care, more likely to die without pain, and family members have less anxiety, depression, and improved quality of life.
- "Palliative" is a term used in the medical field and beyond to describe care approaches that focus on improving the quality of life for patients with a life-threatening illness and their families. It aims to relieve suffering by identifying, assessing,

---
[146] Butler, Katy. The Art of Dying Well: A Practical Guide to a Good End of Life (p. 7). Scribner. Kindle Edition.

and treating pain and other physical, psychosocial, and spiritual problems.

- One of the few studies that included individuals with dementia and their families found five themes around end-of-life choices: Individuals and families wished to avoid dehumanizing treatment and care; they wanted support in confronting emotionally difficult conversations; they needed assistance in navigating existential tension; they needed guidance in defining personal autonomy; and finally, they wanted direction in the face of their lack of confidence in the healthcare system. When PLWD and their families prepare well, they often get to a place of appreciation.
- There is a relatively predictable late-stage course of dementia that can be used to guide contemplation and decisions about when to shift from medical to supportive care only.
- People living with dementia want to know options for assisted death. Most do not choose this course, but many want to know and understand the options.

Action Plan

- Understand that while no one can "plan" death, having no plan will likely leave you with a death that you do not want.
- Sit in quiet contemplation of your reactions to adopting a palliative approach to your care, now and as you move forward in the journey of dementia.
- Sit in contemplation on the five end-of-life themes that were found by others living with dementia and how they resonate with you. The themes are wishing to avoid dehumanizing

treatment and care; wanting support in confronting emotionally difficult conversations; needing assistance in navigating existential tension; needing guidance in defining personal autonomy; and finally, wanting direction in the face of their lack of confidence in the healthcare system.

- Are you curious about assisted death? Consider watching the documentary on assisted death, *Choosing to Die*, or listening the interview with author Amy Bloom hosted by the Hasting Center on her experience with her husband's recent choice to use Dignitas for his death from dementia.

Resources

Wendy Mitchell with Anna Wharton, *Somebody I Used to Know*

In this memoir, Wendy Mitchell, a National Health Service employee, describes her life once diagnosed with young-onset dementia (at age 57). Her blog posts and interviews by Anna Wharton weave together her recognition that she has dementia, how it affects her day-to-day, focusing on leaning into her strengths and facing the reality of her functional decline. She tells a brave story of adapting to her changes and advocating and educating on dementia and preparing for what that means for the person and their supports.

Katy Butler, *The Art of Dying Well: A Practical Guide to a Good End of Life*

Katy Butler, a journalist and end-of-life speaker, provides guidance on how to live well with a chronic medical condition, navigate the complex healthcare system, and increase the likelihood of having a peaceful and well-supported end-of-life. She offers practical steps in her handbook that can be followed to prepare for the end of life whether that be a long way off or just around the corner.

Chapter 9

LEGAL CONSIDERATIONS

The Kenny Family Story

I set the stage before the conversation began. I made sure it was mid-morning, the best time for my mom and her attention and alertness. I made sure my kids were with their other grandmother, happy and entertained. I turned off my cell phone. I turned off my mom's phone and asked her if she was willing to have a deep conversation with me. She said she was, and so we began. As we sipped some tea, I told her I'd been thinking about death, and was hoping she'd be willing to talk to me about that. She chuckled a little and said that I always was thinking about death a little. I told her that it was a shock when my dad died suddenly, and that although I didn't want to be so direct, I wondered if she had thought about what she would want if she didn't die in her sleep, as he did. I told her I wanted to respect her wishes and make sure events unfolded in the way that she wanted them to.

She sat in quiet contemplation for a little bit. Then she said, "I have to admit, I've been thinking about this since this diagnosis. In my work as a clown at the long-term care facilities, I saw so many people who could no longer take care of themselves and just seemed so unhappy. Of course, there were glimmers of smiles or connection, but so many just seemed unhappy and feeling lost. Honestly, I'm scared that that may happen."

"Then let's talk about what sounds like a plan for what would work for you."

We spent the next hour talking quietly about what gave my mom meaning – time with family, laughing, making her own choices as long as possible. She talked about not wanting to be kept alive once she was no longer smiling more than frowning, and if she was fearful all the time of when her body could no longer move around. She said that she wanted hospice involved early. Finally, she told me to trust my instincts if she stopped giving me signals.

We finished our tea, knowing that we had a good plan. And we went to play with the kids – the thing that made her happiest of all!

Overview

Why do we need the legal decisions and documents in place? Wendy Mitchell, a person living with dementia and author of *Somebody I Used to Know*, describes her fears. "[It's the] same three things that whittle away inside, and each time the thought of one creeps in, the other two leap to join it. The fear of losing my independence, of being unable to get a bus to and from town, let alone work. I glance at my ghostly reflection in the bus window, a reminder of another major fear: going over the edge into someone I don't recognize, losing a grip on what makes me. A time when decisions will be made for me, not by me. And then that naturally leads to the third fear, so painful that each time it comes to me I feel my heart twist in response; forgetting the faces of the two people who are most dear to me, Sarah and Gemma [her daughters]."[147]

To make sound legal and financial decisions, it's important to consider your values, your aspirations, and what matters to you personally. This can lead to deep and meaningful conversations.

Christine Thelker, a woman living with vascular dementia and author of *For This I Am Grateful: Living with Dementia*, wrote, "Everyday, if I feel good, I'm doing what I can to enjoy this day, this hour, right now, and on days when I am not feeling right, I rest. Giving into this has been a challenge; I'm so used to multitasking, making decisions, taking care of others, it's hard to realize I am not able to do it all, that it's okay to just BE sometimes. I'm always ready for the worst, hoping for the best, hoping to tackle my bucket list, wondering if the neurologist can actually do anything, or am I just slipping away little by little. I have lots of hard decisions coming up and wonder how I will wade through them when my brain is not what it was."[148]

Christine Thelker is a widow and has no children. She realizes she will be making many decisions and doing much of her bucket list alone. "Perhaps after more doctor's appointments, I will be better able to make more decisions; for right now, it overwhelms me. Sometimes it makes me sad, sometimes it makes

---

[147] Mitchell, Wendy. Somebody I Used to Know (p. 71). Random House Publishing Group. Kindle Edition
[148] Christine Thelker, For This I Am Grateful, p 48

me crazy, but mostly it makes me try to enjoy each and every day to whatever degree I can. I am hopeful today."[149]

Christine, at a later point in the book, finds a study about meaning-based psychotherapy conducted by Gary Breitbart. "The time between diagnosis and death, he found, presents an opportunity for 'extraordinary growth' ... meaning in life ... and that realization ultimately brought ... some measure of peace and consolation as they faced life's final challenge. ... There is still so much I want to do, see, experience."[150]

Estates and Finances

"I have always been a very decisive person ... making decisions then getting on with it; except now my brain doesn't want to make a decision. Another frustration. Today I will challenge my brain to start building a plan and putting it on paper."[151]

It may be beneficial to create legal documents that detail how your estate and finances will be managed in the future. These documents could include a will, durable power of attorney for finances, or a living trust, depending on your specific needs and situation.

A *will* is a legal document that outlines how your assets, including property, money and other belongings, will be distributed and managed after you die. It can also make provisions for the care of your children under age 18, adult dependents, and pets. Additionally, a will can specify your end-of-life arrangements such as your funeral or memorial service and burial or

---

[149] Christine Thelker, For This I Am Grateful, p 46
[150] Christine Thelker, *For This I Am Grateful*, p 48
[151] Christine Thelker, *For This I Am Grateful*, p 45

cremation. If you do not have a will, your estate will be distributed according to the laws in your state.

"My lawyer and I sat down and tackled the daunting task of getting things in order ... my will rewritten first. I wonder if people realize they should have one ... they are so important ... not because of money or stuff but because when someone dies, it is such a difficult task to get through the day never mind trying to navigate all that has to be done. A will simplifies many things for those left behind. By writing a will, you're actually giving those you left in charge of your affairs the gift of easing an otherwise daunting task. Wills should be reviewed from time to time, so they are current. Mine is now current. I also have all my power of attorney papers in order."[152]

A *durable power of attorney for finances* designates an individual to make financial decisions on your behalf in the event that you are unable to do so.

A *living trust* is a legal document that designates a trustee to manage and distribute your property and funds if you become unable to handle your affairs.

It might be a good idea to discuss with a lawyer the options of creating a general or durable power of attorney, joint account, or trust. Make sure to inquire about the lawyer's fees beforehand. To find local lawyers, you can search online, contact your local library or bar association for lawyers, or use the Eldercare Locator.[153] Your state's free legal aid options can be found through your local bar association. If necessary, consult with a knowledgeable family member.

---
152 Christine Thelker, For *This I Am Grateful*, p 46
153 https://eldercare.acl.gov/Public/Index.aspx

Planning for Healthcare

Christine Thelker says, "So many things are different now; I didn't even realize until I started on the Aricept, how in so many ways I was not managing as well as I had thought. For sure I had friends around me who compensated for me. Bless their hearts. My family and friends ensured that nothing totally devastating happened. I have come to the realization that if I am to write and try to help others along this journey it is going to take some brutal honesty on my part. In a sense it's like taking the mask off, being real, being vulnerable."[154]

To ensure that your medical wishes are followed in case you become unable to communicate decisions due to illness or injury, you can prepare advance directives. These legal documents, such as a living will or durable power of attorney for health care, only come into effect under those circumstances.

A living will is a document that informs doctors about the medical treatment you want in case you are unable to make decisions in case you are unable to make decisions for yourself. You can specify the medical treatments and care you prefer, the ones you don't want, and the conditions under which these choices apply.

A durable power of attorney for health care allows you to appoint someone as your health care proxy. The proxy acts on your behalf in making health care decisions if you are unable to communicate. It is important for the proxy to be well-aware of your values and desires. This proxy can be chosen in addition to or instead of a living will. Having a health care proxy is useful in unpredictable situations like a severe accident or stroke.

---
154 Christine Thelker, For This I Am Grateful, p 48

LEGAL CONSIDERATIONS

While you may want to employ a lawyer in creating a durable power of attorney for healthcare, creating advance directives for healthcare does not necessarily require a lawyer. In fact, free forms are available in most states and can be filled out by individuals themselves.

Keep Your Papers Accessible

To keep your important papers and legal documents organized and easily accessible, you have a few options. You can create a designated file, store them in a desk or dresser drawer, or list their location and information in a notebook. For extra protection, it may be wise to invest in a fireproof and waterproof safe to store your documents. If your papers are in a bank safe deposit box, it's a good idea to keep copies at home.

There are books that will help you gather these papers together. If you employ a lawyer, financial advisor, or accountant, they may have a secured digital vault that can store copies of your paperwork in one place, or you can find something similar such as MyDataDiary+[155] which does have a one-time fee. Make sure that your designated decision maker knows where to find these documents and has access to the password.

---

155 mydatadiary.com

Table 2: Common Documents Needed

What Papers Do I Need	
Personal information	• Full legal name • Social Security number • Legal residence • Date and place of birth • Names and addresses of spouse and children • Location of birth and death certificates and certificates of marriage, divorce, citizenship, and adoption • Employers and dates of employment • Education and military records • Names and phone numbers of religious contacts • Memberships in groups and awards received • Names and phone numbers of close friends, relatives, doctors, lawyers, and financial advisors

LEGAL CONSIDERATIONS

Financial information	• Sources of income and assets (pension from your employer, IRAs, 401(k)s, interest, etc.) • Social Security information • Pension information • Insurance information (life, long-term care, home, car) with policy numbers and agents' names and phone numbers • Names of your banks and account numbers (checking, savings, credit union) • Investment income (stocks, bonds, property) and stockbrokers' names and phone numbers • Copy of most recent income tax return • Location of most up-to-date will with an original signature • Liabilities, including property tax –what is owed, to whom, and when payments are due • Mortgages and debts –how and when they are paid • Location of original deed of trust for home • Car title and registration • Credit and debit card names and numbers • Location of safe deposit box and key

Health information	• Current prescriptions (be sure to update this regularly) • Living will • Durable power of attorney for health care • Copies of any medical or order forms you have (for example, a do-not-resuscitate order or POLST/MOLST) • Health insurance information with policy and phone numbers, including Medicare and Medicaid.

Let Someone Know Where to Find Important Documents

Let a trusted person know where to find the above documents and information. This might include family members, your lawyer, or other professionals helping you manage your estate. Provide them with passwords (if using online tools) in case they need access to something on their own. Make sure someone can help carry out your wishes if something happens to you.

In case of an emergency or cognitive loss, it is important to let someone you trust or a lawyer know the location of your important documents. You do not need to disclose personal information, but it is essential that someone knows where to find your papers. If you do not have a trustworthy friend or relative, you can seek assistance from a lawyer.

Have the Discussions

It's important to discuss advance care planning with both your doctor and your family members. Your doctor can help you

LEGAL CONSIDERATIONS

anticipate future health decisions and determine what kind of care or treatment you would prefer. Medicare covers these discussions for free during your annual wellness visit, and private health insurance may also cover them. By sharing your decisions with your family members, you can prevent any unexpected situations or misunderstandings about your wishes.

"I will not go into any type of long-term care, private or public. I know so, so many loving, kind, caring, and compassionate people who truly do amazing jobs in these facilities, they truly love those they care for, those people are truly a gift to all. But I also know there are many who should not be working on those types of units, in those positions, whether they are the RN, LPN, Care Aid, housekeeper, food service workers, whatever. The system allows them to continue working long beyond what is acceptable. I've always been a loud voice for this to change."[156] For this wish to be realized, Christine needs to have her plans, her advocate, her physicians to be clear on the plan as her dementia progresses. She needs to have an in-home plan, and hospice ready or a plan to decide to stop eating and drinking or a trip to Dignatas in her future.

You can authorize a doctor or lawyer to communicate with your caregiver by granting advanced permission. If you require assistance with your care, you can allow your caregiver to converse with your doctors, lawyer, insurance provider, credit card company, or bank. It may be necessary to sign a form and return it. Bear in mind that authorizing your doctor or lawyer to speak to your caregiver is not the same as appointing a health care proxy. A health care proxy can only make decisions if you become incapable of making these decisions yourself.

---

156 Christine Thelker, *For This I Am Grateful*, p 54

Review and Update Your Plans Regularly

It is important to review your plans on a yearly basis and whenever a significant life event takes place, such as a divorce, relocation, or major health issue.

Other Considerations

Organ Donation

When a person passes away, their healthy organs and tissues can be donated to help others who need them. You can register to be an organ donor when you renew your driver's license or state ID at your local motor vehicle department or online. Additionally, some people choose to donate their brains for scientific research. It is possible to donate organs for transplant and the brain for research purposes.

Funeral Plans

It's possible to plan your funeral or memorial service in advance by choosing the type of service and the location. You can also decide whether you prefer burial or cremation and what should be done with the ashes – whether to keep them with loved ones or scatter them in a meaningful place. It's important to specify any religious, spiritual, or cultural traditions you want to be incorporated into your visitation, funeral, or memorial service. To make arrangements, reach out to a funeral home or crematory directly.

Planning in advance for your funeral can assist you in making well-informed and considerate decisions regarding the funeral services you prefer. This enables you to choose the specific items that are needed and desired, as well as compare the prices

LEGAL CONSIDERATIONS

offered by various funeral providers. Additionally, pre-planning saves your loved ones from the burden of having to make these decisions while dealing with time constraints and overwhelming emotions. Directly contacting a funeral establishment can assist you in making these arrangements.

It is important to plan ahead for funerals and consider the location for burying, entombing, or scattering a loved one's remains. Typically, family members are rushed to buy a cemetery plot without careful consideration or a personal visit to the site in the short time between the death and burial. Therefore, it is best to purchase cemetery plots before they are needed to ensure the family's best interests are met.

It is advisable to plan your arrangements ahead of time but avoid making advanced payments. Please note that prices may increase, and businesses may close or change ownership as time passes. However, in some areas where there is high competition, prices may decrease over time. It is recommended that you review and update your decisions every few years and inform your family of your wishes.

There is also a movement to make burial more energy efficient or 'green'. A vast amount of information can be found at Green Burial Council.[157] Green burial is currently legal in Washington, Oregon, California, Minnesota, Vermont, Colorado, and New York with legislation pending in Massachusetts, Maryland, Illinois, and Maine.

Advance Care Planning

Not everyone is ready to have conversations about advance care planning. For them, I often ask them to do some homework.

---
[157] https://www.greenburialcouncil.org/

I highly recommend the Conversation Project guide[158] from the Institute for Healthcare Improvement, founded by Ellen Goodman and Len Fishman. The guide provides a process to begin these difficult and often taboo conversations about medical and legal decisions regarding death. The guide focuses on values and wishes to guide those who need help in making end-of-life decisions. These conversations are crucial to being able to complete advance directives with confidence and without fear.

Advance directives are written instructions that provide information on your goals and wishes if you're seriously ill, dying, or living with a long-term chronic, disabling condition. Sometimes referred to as a living will, this aspect of advanced planning focuses specifically on resuscitation, intubation, and feeding at the end of life.

There are several websites that are excellent in assisting someone in understanding and creating a living will. This can also be done with a physician or a lawyer. The websites that I recommend highly are the Conversation Project,[159] Compassion and Choices,[160] Prepare for your Care,[161] and the Five Wishes.[162] Please realize that if you would like to use these websites as a guide for supplemental information and expanding the discussion, you do not want to negate the legal documents you may have filled out with a lawyer. Ask your lawyer to add language to your current document as necessary or use the examples from the preferred website and make it clear that these choices are an addendum to be added to your legally

---

158 https://theconversationproject.org/
159 https://theconversationproject.org/
160 https://www.compassionandchoices.org/
161 https://prepareforyourcare.org/en/welcome
162 https://www.fivewishes.org/

drafted document. If there are two conflicting documents, the most recent document is the one that will be upheld, but you do not want confusion about your end-of-life choices, as it will result in stress, emotional upheaval to your family, and possibly unwanted therapies.

The living will is obviously limited in scope, as there are so many decisions that need to be made when someone has a cognitive loss and has lost the ability to make day-to-day decisions. For this reason, a healthcare proxy or a durable power of attorney is needed by anyone living with cognitive loss. This person should be someone whom you trust to follow your wishes and directives. If your family cannot help you with this due to their own inability to deal with death and dying, it may be worthwhile to pick someone else. I feel that most families, if given enough time and attention to their own distress, can fulfill this support role, but it is very personal. A durable power of attorney must be someone 18 years old or older, and the person does not have to be a family member. A lawyer is not required to establish a durable power of attorney but should probably be consulted if you plan to establish one. There are nuances that should be considered about what authorities you will relinquish and when.

"I have witnessed time and time again, family, caregivers, nursing staff come all insisting that a person is fed even when it is clear this is no longer a viable action. I believe it is done because people have the need 'to do something' when clearly a person doesn't want any more to be done. Many times, the body is trying to shut down and we are forcing it to do unnatural things during that process. Really, we should be giving them comfort, respect, relief from pain, and allowing their bodies to do what is natural.[163]

I highly recommend reviewing your living will and health-care proxy on an annual basis. You need to make sure that none of these arrangements are changing as you notice new developments with your disease. Pick a time that works for you. Some people batch this review with their taxes, as that is a time when legal and financial reviews are happening. Others link to a less hectic time of year. It is important to review and revise as needed.

A More Complete Living Will for Those Living with Dementia

In Chapter 8, we discussed what the end of dementia may look like, and we further discussed if someone wanted to explore options for limiting their life.

Advance care planning about refusing treatment in the future is also possible. Beyond just limiting resuscitation and/or ventilation, individuals can refuse medical treatment of chronic conditions, blood transfusions, trips to the hospital (with a caveat if desired to allow exceptions for trauma), antibiotics, and hand or tube feeding.

There is literature, mostly out of Susan Mitchell's team at Harvard University,[164] that documents the futility and increased harm that continued medication, hydration, hospitalization, antibiotics, and other medical interventions cause when someone has moved beyond living well with dementia and has begun to die from dementia.

---

163 Christine Thelker, *For This I Am Grateful*, p 46
164 https://hms.harvard.edu/faculty-staff/susan-mitchell

LEGAL CONSIDERATIONS

There are specialized advance care plans that outline some of these special circumstances and may guide you in thinking through some of the more complex choices at the end of life. Of the many I've reviewed, I like the Compassion and Choices resources specific to dementia.[165] They have a toolkit that has logical choices for therapies that can sustain life. Further there is a dementia-specific addendum that outlines care preferences, such as I want to live as long as possible; I want no life-saving treatments; keep me comfortable, and stop or avoid any treatments that are preventing me from dying from other diseases; keep me comfortable while stopping all treatments and withholding food and water so that I can die peacefully.

The document also outlines 14 markers of progression of the disease so that these care preferences can coincide with the marker. The markers of progression include items such as "I am angry or violent and it is not controlled with medication"; "I can no longer communicate with my loved ones through words"; "I can no longer leave my bed"; and "the only option to care for me is in a nursing home."

"I was reading a very interesting article by a doctor in New Zealand who specializes in dementia care. I am so glad there are doctors like him. I will be discussing some of what he talks about with my own doctors. He suggests when the disease has progressed to a certain point doctors should stop all other medications, like cholesterol, blood pressure, heart meds and only give and focus on things that will provide comfort. Don't treat pneumonia; don't do surgeries for broken hips, etc. None of those things will change the outcome. Today I am still well enough to be treated but the day is coming when that will not

---
165 to b added

be the case. Prolonging life should not be considered at a certain point; I would rather be able to die naturally without the 'doctoring' than have to endure living in any of our so-called 'homes.'"[166]

Communication with Others

It is imperative that your family, advocates, and healthcare providers understand your wishes. I believe it is important enough to warrant Chapter 4 Communication and Communication Changes.

But to complete this chapter, remember to have frequent (at least annual) conversations with your family and physician. The first time is the most robust and difficult. From then on, it can merely be a touchstone – reminding them that you've put thought into these decisions and ask that they continue to support the decision.

Points to Remember

- Use the values and reflections that you've worked on in previous chapters to guide your legal and financial decisions about current and end-of-life choices.
- It may be beneficial to create legal documents that detail how your estate and finances will be managed in the future. These documents could include a will, durable power of attorney for finances, or a living trust, depending on your specific needs and situation.
- A living will, expanded choices about end-of-life care, and a durable power of attorney are crucial to having a system

---

166 Christine Thelker, *For This I Am Grateful*, p 98

LEGAL CONSIDERATIONS

in place to ensure that your life ends in a way that is meaningful to you.
- Paperwork can and should be gathered now. Table 1 offers a checklist to follow. Take it a section at a time.

Action Plan

- Review your values and goals for estate, financial, and healthcare needs and desires.
- If you do not have a durable power of attorney, a will, or advance directives, find an experienced elder law attorney and make an appointment to have these documents prepared.
- Choose a system to gather your documents – it could be as simple as a folder or more complex with a digital "vault." Choose one and begin to gather or photocopy needed documents.
- Inform your durable power of attorney where all these documents (and passwords) are held.
- Review a Compassion and Choices dementia-specific addendum[167] to your living will to guide you in making some value-based choices on dementia-specific life choices.
- Schedule a talk with your family or, at a minimum, whomever is chosen as having durable power of attorney.

---

167 https://www.compassionandchoices.org/

Resources

Christine Thelker, *For This I am Grateful: Living with Dementia.*

Ms. Thelker writes about being diagnosed with vascular dementia at age 55 years. She tells her story of finding the resources she needed to cope and adapt to her diagnosis and limitations, leaning heavily into her strengths. She then found new hope and purpose in her connection with Dementia Alliance International, an organization of people living with dementia which sparked more strengths.

Catherine Hodder, Esq., *Estate Planning for the Sandwich Generation: How to Help Your Parents and Protect Your Kids.*

A pragmatic overview of legal aspects of estate planning. A quick primer to exposure to the documents, types of wills and trusts, and common needs to get paperwork in order. A review of a book such as this can make the trip to the lawyer to implement many aspects of estate planning less overwhelming, be used as a refresher guide after that appointment, and leave you feeling a bit more knowledgeable about legalese.

Chapter 10

ENGAGING WITH FAMILY AND THE HEALTHCARE SYSTEM

The Kenny Family Story

My mom was in the early stages of her dementia, but overall had good judgment. She was married to her second husband, who also was showing signs of cognitive loss. At first, they did well together – Mom reminded him to take his medications, he warned her when food seemed "off" as she had lost her sense of smell (a not uncommon condition that accompanies cognitive loss). Being together reminded the other to eat and provided structure in their days. But both extended families were noticing that unsafe activities were beginning to occur. For example, their car broke down due to unattended maintenance. They were both dressed for spring, though temperatures were freezing. They waited for the tow truck outside of the car, and both were at high risk for hypothermia when my sister came upon them. Soon after this incident, my mother's husband required hospitalization for heart failure. His family, concerned about the multiple warning signs from their father that his cognition and overall health were declining and that my mother was faltering as a caregiver, decided to have him admitted to a long-term care facility. This, of course, prompted discussions with Mom about whether she would like to move to a more social, more structured living situation. Mom thought she would like to continue to live home alone.

My sister and brother increased their visits to support her in this decision. My mom would call my sister-in-law, who was home during the day, to report that it had taken her all day to visit the long-term care facility – we pieced together that she had been lost and driving for hours. She began visiting the bank nearly daily as fears about her finances mounted. The "angel" from the bank informed my sister. My mother had repeated visits to the emergency department for diarrhea and abdominal pain, which we discovered came from eating tainted food that she did not recognize as spoiled due to her loss of smell and cognitive loss. The trial at living independently was not going well. My mom was upset with us. She was in a free fall after losing her husband to dementia, stepfamily drama, a change in living situation, the death of her son, her own cognitive loss, and now, the loss of her independence. She understood the situation had become untenable, but that did not stop her feelings of anger, loss, frustration, and fear. My siblings and I, too, felt a deep loss. We had to step in and force the issue of moving to a more structured living environment. The visits to potential assisted living facilities were often done in near silence with no smiles, no positive comments, no joy. My mother usually looked for the silver lining in all situations. We were trying to incorporate her wishes with what seemed an undeniable reality. She *was clear she did not want to live with any of us, but she was also clear she wanted to continue to live alone. Assisted living seemed the best choice, as she would have her own apartment, but there would be activities, socialization, and medical support outside the door. Safe food and socialization for meals would be provided, and her ability to do light cooking would be maintained. She complied, but was very angry with us, and with her situation. Thankfully, she was able to communicate her anger, her fear, and her disappointment to all of us, as she also faced the changes that the functional loss from dementia was bringing.*

Overview

Many individuals will be living alone with cognitive loss. The numbers are increasing. An estimated 4.3 million older adults with cognitive impairment live alone in the United States[168]. Findings from a study[169] regarding people with early cognitive loss who were living alone generated a series of questions which I think are worth pondering as you decide how to communicate your wishes, wants, needs, and desires with your family or your healthcare providers. This is possibly more important as you explore what may be needed, as you may not be able to know or see what is coming, and you've never lived this experience before. The questions, modified by me to frame how you can ask for help, support, and ideas from your family, friends, or healthcare team, include:

---

[168] Edwards, RD, Brenowitz, WD, Portacolone, E, et al. Difficulty and help with activities of daily living among older adults living alone with cognitive impairment. *Alzheimer's Dement.* 2020; 16: 1125–1133. https://doi.org/10.1002/alz.12102

[169] Elena Portacolone, MPH, MBA, PhD and others, The Precarity of Older Adults Living Alone With Cognitive Impairment, *The Gerontologist*, Volume 59, Issue 2, April 2019, Pages 271–280, https://doi.org/10.1093/geront/gnx193

- How can help and support alleviate my psychological distress as I live alone (or with others) with cognitive impairment?
- How can family/friends and others support me so that I can stay in my home?
- What services would improve my quality of life?
- How can family, friends, healthcare workers tailor these services to my degree of cognitive impairment, particularly as my abilities decline over time?
- How can these services also be tailored to the diverse needs of mine – whether that is my ethnic/racial background, residence in a rural or urban area, or other circumstances?

The study indicated that individuals who live alone expressed dissatisfaction with those who will assist and who did not fully comprehend their needs and preferences. On the other hand, those who could assist mentioned the difficulties of offering assistance to people with limited resources or resistance. It is important to consider the perspective of individuals who live alone when creating professional guidelines, as they often face unrealistic demands.

Gerda Saunders, a woman living with cognitive loss and author of *Memory's Last Breath*, describes her feelings soon after her diagnosis when she is looking for answers, direction, and assistance. "In the days after my neurologist gave a name to what was wrong with me, the separate circles in which I had kept the images of myself as a woman who lives and dies by her rationality and that of my mother after her illness as a Dickensian madwoman gradually began to overlap like the intersection of a Venn diagram. Within that convergence, I came out to myself in tones that sounded believable to my skeptical ears: I am dementing. I am dementing. I am dementing."[170]

How best, then, to manage to relieve the burden of self-managing one's cognitive impairment?

The Problem with Building a Team

Many living with cognitive loss describe a feeling of precarity, or uncertainty. "The notion of precarity evokes an intrinsic sense of uncertainty resulting from coping with cumulative pressures while trying to preserve a sense of independence."[171] The article, which featured interviews with several individuals living with cognitive loss, found that many individuals felt a burden to manage their disease, to be "careful." A Tattoo on the Brain author, Dr. Daniel Gibbs, mentions that he must fight apathy, that he has to push through feelings of laziness, that he cannot look too far forward in his disease or he will falter. Gerda Saunders feels it is important for all to know the good and the bad of dementia so that we can make an impact – either as one living with or one supporting others – always with love. "Like Bayley [Bayley is the spouse of famous author Iris Murdoch who developed dementia in her later years], I myself tell tales out of school in order to expose the unsavory realities of dementia, and I come down on the side of those who believe that through his shocking disclosures combined with his unfailing care "Bayley demonstrates how love still thrives in such uncompromising familiarity [and that] this book reveals itself

---

170 Saunders, Gerda. Memory's Last Breath (p. 13). Hachette Books. Kindle Edition.
171 Portacolone E, Rubinstein RL, Covinsky KE, Halpern J, Johnson JK. The Precarity of Older Adults Living Alone With Cognitive Impairment. Gerontologist. 2019 Mar 14;59(2):271-280

as one brave enough to face such ambivalence as well as the horror of dementia."[172]

But, how to be "careful" without giving up all your rights and freedoms? This puts you in a precarious situation on decisions as well – how to ask for help, but not receive too much help? How to put safeguards into place, but not have those assisting you "take over"?

Gerda Saunders reveals a time when this back-and-forth due to her cognitive loss made work much more difficult. "A new working method soon arose from the gyre of perplexity in which I was trapped: when my task spawned a question, I wrote it down on a worksheet in longhand before switching to the reference screen, so the query would not slip my mind once I got there. The corollary also held once I found the answer, I jotted it down before returning to my draft. (This tedious method still serves me well as I write this book.) The most stressful aspect of the process was the epochs, eras, eons it ate away in slow motion. For the first time in my life, I had to delegate some of my other responsibilities to already overworked colleagues in order to meet our deadlines. While I did manage to deliver the policies on time and well-enough written that my colleagues approved them with only minor changes, my ego was in shreds."[173]

Living alone, strategies are often relying on notes, but many individuals are concerned that they cannot remember where the note is. When my mother lived alone, she had piles of mail, papers, and notes. She would sort through them over and over again. The piles were both a source of stress for her and a source of anxiety relief. I would ask her about it as we

---
172 Saunders, Gerda. Memory's Last Breath (p. 60). Hachette Books. Kindle
173 Saunders, Gerda. Memory's Last Breath (p. 67). Hachette Books. Kindle Edition.

sorted through her pile together when I visited. I would attempt to help her file some of the papers, make sure that bills were paid or automated, but that did not stop her worry that she had forgotten one of them and the sorting would begin again. The pressure of keeping track of all of it in the face of memory loss and living alone caused undue anxiety. I wish I could have taken this burden from her, but she wanted to remain independent in her finances. What I learned from this aspect of my mother's and my journey with dementia, I would have asked to be more directly helpful in aspects of her life that were too difficult and caused her undue stress and allowed her more time focusing on areas of strength, joy and happiness.

Individuals living with dementia report increased anxiety about whether they remember the note or not. And often, feel frustration that services not tailored to the myriad of issues that come up to care for themselves, their homes, their finances, their transportation, and their socialization, especially when also faced with cognitive loss. Individuals living with dementia realize that if they request help, their family and friends may then overdo or overreact. And they are likely correct. Families and healthcare providers often focus on safety above all else, rather than negotiated risk, balancing values and quality of life with safety.

This area will be continually changing as individuals with cognitive loss advocate for their own rights and society begins to listen to their voice – your voice.

Facilitated Discussion with Family

I believe it comes down to open and honest communication – something that not everyone can do but a goal worth striving for.

The guidelines must be set – the focus cannot be just safety or the discussion won't happen. To be the most safe, likely, everyone with cognitive loss would need to enter a structured care setting or not live alone, since we never know when one day the gaps or befuddled experiences may occur. Can you find someone that would facilitate this discussion? Someone you trust with experience facilitating a crowd that may have differing opinions? Someone who can hold a safe container for all to speak, contribute, and be heard. Someone who can coax out some of the underlying messages that are being spoken? A few suggestions are clergy, a social worker, a geriatric case manager or a therapist. Find someone neutral, but with some understanding of dementia and autonomy.

How can you prepare to fill in the gaps when you live alone? As the disease progresses, issues will arise in executive function.

How to address them? When to know that it is time to layer in support or change the living situation? Can some guideposts be discussed, and when they are hit, understand that movement will be needed.

The character Alice in the Lisa Genova novel *Still Alice* set up a series of tests which she performed daily to remind her to begin a premeditated death plan for when she could no longer execute that series of test. I don't quite agree with the "tasks" she set forth as her marker or that she chose not to

ENGAGING WITH FAMILY AND THE HEALTHCARE SYSTEM

share these discussions with anyone else, but the point is, what can be identified objectively now (e.g., unable to take medications independently), while executive function is going well, that can be discussed with others and assessed intermittently, and can support or actions be agreed upon or planned for when the function fails (e.g., allowed a technology-enhanced pillbox to distribute pills and notify family if the pills are not removed or a move to assisted living with medication support)?

The MacArthur Foundation coalesced information from a host of research regarding competence to devise a clinical framework for assessing competence You and your family can use these questions to assist in decision making in areas where you or they are concerned that your ability or safety are in question. The questions have been used to help researchers decide if one is able to provide consent for research protocols and that clinicians can use to assist when someone living with dementia is facing decisions regarding medical/psychosocial interventions.

Families could use this framework as well. This interview is known as the MacArthur Competence Assessment Tool (Mac-CAT).[174] The questions that are asked are:

- Does the person have the ability to understand facts?
- Do they recognize how these facts affect the risk and benefits to daily living?
- What would happen if the intervention was chosen or refused?

---

[174] Grisso T, Appelbaum PS. Assessing Competence to Consent to Treatment: A Guide for Physicians and other Health Care Professionals (Oxford Press).

- And what would be their choice, given the above information?

Can you identify someone who can then be appointed to implement the plan for you? What happens if you don't? Likely there will be a crisis or emergency where others will step in, and your choices may be taken away from you. Adult Protective Services may be called, and your independence and freedoms will be curtailed. Or you will be left to languish, increasing your stress and loneliness.

I recommend finding at least one person who can become your ally or advocate in understanding your vision for a balance between safety and freedom. Can that one person align with you to build a team that will honor these wishes?

Who is on Your Team? How Can You Enhance It?

Many who are told they are living with cognitive loss receive recommendations to build a team, but how? There are several steps that will help.

Inventory

Begin with an inventory of who is on your team already and begin to communicate clearly with them. The first order of business is asking them to help in building and organizing the larger team. Unfortunately, dementia can most severely affect building and organizing skills, so it is important to shore up this aspect of the team.

There are several people who may be able to help with this aspect, but sometimes it is wise to bring in a coach or expert if it is financially feasible. Someone with expertise in dementia care or a geriatric case manager, though expensive, can be used to set up the team and then come in only occasionally to make sure things stay on track. Other options include contacting the Area Agency on Aging for advice on services, your town social worker, or the social worker associated with your physician's office.

Let it Happen

As with many aspects of dealing with dementia, the first step is a shift in our mindsets. We don't ask for help for a host of reasons. We often feel weak when we ask for help. Joan Halifax, Ph.D., a Buddhist monk, performs an exercise where a person is blindfolded and led by another on a walk.[175] Each person takes a turn leading and being led. When led, people notice they feel weak and feeble. It's understandable that you are reluctant to ask for help then ... if it makes you feel weak.

Now, let's reframe that. Sit quietly for a few minutes and recall when you have been asked for help by another. How did you feel? Honored to be asked? Excited that your gifts and talents are appreciated? Loved so much by the other that they had the courage to ask you? And when the other thanked you for your help, were you filled by the gratitude and appreciation expressed? Most people feel good helping others – it brings out feelings of strength, openness, and love.

With this reflection and list of benefits, acknowledge that asking others can be a benefit to them and resolve to let their help in.

---

[175] Halifax, J *Being with Dying*

Think of Your Team as Layers of Support or Teams of Support

With the help of those in your inner circle or the hired coach/professional, begin to brainstorm other sources of help and assistance. Think broadly and consider the support as ever-expanding layers. Who is closest and most likely to help – in what ways? Once you have a list of people or tasks that need to be done, the lists can be more finely tuned.

Brainstorm the names of others whom you believe would like to help to varying degrees, such as other friends and family members, neighbors, social club members, or those related to any religious organization with whom you have an association. Brainstorming can be done alone, but I bring it forward now so that you gather the closest "other" with you, to make it a group activity as one member's idea may trigger another idea from the group! Brainstorming is the process of rapidly generating ideas to solve a problem or think in a new way. There are a few helpful rules:

1) Think of as many ideas as you can – the key is quantity!
2) Withhold criticism – the point of the exercise is to expand thinking.
3) Wild ideas are welcome here – it is easier to rein in a wild idea than to expand a simple idea.
4) Combine ideas to spur the generation of even more ideas.

Widen your circle to healthcare providers (primary care provider (PCP); medical specialist; physical, speech, or occupational therapist; dentist; optometrist; podiatrist; healthcare coach; nutritionist; psychologist or mental health therapist), home-care agencies, and hospice agencies.

Move out in your layers to non-medical providers such as financial advisors, accountants, bankers, social workers, care managers, and other service providers such as personal care companies.

Finally, identify other resources that may be available to assist like cleaning services, personal chefs or meal preparation services like Meals on Wheels, personal shoppers, virtual administrators, transportation companies, administrators/computer users, technology expertise, handyman services, and lawn care services.

Where Will You Likely Need Assistance?

Among individuals with dementia, the ability to live alone is dependent on physical ability and cognitive capacity to perform daily activities independently. Studies reveal that individuals with dementia who lived alone had significantly more unmet needs than those living with others, particularly in the areas of looking after home, food preparation, self-care, and accidental self-harm.[176] It is the instrumental activities of daily living that we must make sure are addressed first (see Chapter 2 for a review of instrumental activities of daily living and activities of daily living).

At times, we may live in denial that we are having issues. Be on the lookout for tell-tale signs. These signs include going to the emergency room often, having very little food at home, looking untidy, wearing dirty clothes, and wearing clothes that are not suitable for the weather. You may be able to see this is

---

[176] Miranda-Castillo C, Woods B, Orrell M. People with dementia living alone: what are their needs and what kind of support are they receiving? Int Psychogeriatr. 2010 Jun;22(4):607-17. doi: 10.1017/S104161021000013X. Epub 2010 Mar 10. PMID: 20214844.).

happening but also be aware that someone else may let you know they notice this change.

What kind of help do I even want? Who are they helping? Food (shopping, cooking, prepping)? Cleaning (inside, outside)? Activities? Driving? Medicine? Yard work? Handyperson chores? Emotional support?

Once you have your brainstorming idea done, begin to organize the list around types of help.

Prioritize What Would Be Most Helpful to You from This List in Order of Importance to You:

Where would you get your most benefit? Pick your top three.

Act on one idea from the list and keep it small and doable. Make a plan so that you know the who, what, when, and why of your ask.

Consider this building your "asking muscle."

Who will you ask for help from the list?

How will you ask them? Phone call, email, text message? What is easiest for you?

Can you script the "ask" so that you can get beyond any nervousness that may come up?

What can happen from here? They say yes and you've begun to build the first person on your caregiving team. Time to celebrate!!

What if they say no? Realize that they are not rejecting you but have to prioritize their own lives. This part can be tough, because none of us likes rejection. But we are not children anymore and we can handle a tiny bit of rejection. Thank them for allowing you to ask and move down your list.

Feel the Success

Once you've found some help, review your list and build another aspect of help. Make this a weekly activity. It will take some time, but by building your team, you will be saving yourself time and energy (physical, emotional, and spiritual) down the road. Maybe you could even ask someone to help you find help, using your list!

Begin the Process (or Find Another) to Organize Your List of Helpers and Tasks

To clarify, after making a list of ideas, it's useful to review and weigh the pros and cons of each before categorizing them. To help with this process, consider creating a document with columns for the names, phone numbers, email addresses, and locations of potential support team members based on category. If you're not comfortable with computers, ask someone who is to help you organize the information to share with others.

What are the Situations that May Need the Help of Friends/Family?

Socialization/Adapting to Cognitive Loss

A 2005 brain imaging study proves what relatives and caretakers of people with dementia have long known: "the sound of a loved one's voice activated widely distributed circuits" in the brains of seriously brain-injured patients, and the most stimulating social environment possible leads to the highest possible levels of lucidity in old age, even in people who "have brains that appear riddled with Alzheimer's disease" or other dementia-type lesions. "Many of them remain social to the end, engaged in regular card games or debates with friends who make mental demands of them.[177]

Peter Berry, a gentleman living with early-onset Alzheimer's disease, remarks in his memoir, written along with his friend Deb Bunt, that he needs a challenge. His challenges often involve his love of biking and his dementia advocacy. He is barely done with one challenge before he is looking to the next, to keep himself engaged. He finds these challenges keep his "dementia monster" at bay.

In studies of people living alone with dementia, the anxiety or concern about handling their day-to-day lives, their houses, and their organization reportedly causes a significant amount of worry.

And loneliness and isolation, caused by stigma, loss of planning, or loss of transportation, can lead to poor quality of life as well. How can a team help with mitigating some of these very common problems or concerns of those living with early dementia?

Goal-oriented cognitive rehabilitation, a structured 10-session meeting done alone or in a group, facilitated by trained occupational therapists or social workers, has been shown to improve "the process of psychological adjustment to living with dementia, leading to feelings of greater confidence, less anxiety, and better coping skills."[178]

---

[177] Saunders, Gerda. Memory's Last Breath (p. 179). Hachette Books. Kindle Edition who also quotes Benedict Carey, "After Injury, Fighting to Regain a Sense of Self," New York Times, August 8, 2009.

[178] Clare L, Kudlicka A, Oyebode JR, Jones RW, Bayer A, Leroi I, Kopelman M, James IA, Culverwell A, Pool J, Brand A, Henderson C, Hoare Z, Knapp M, Morgan-Trimmer S, Burns A, Corbett A, Whitaker R, Woods B. Goal-oriented cognitive rehabilitation for early-stage Alzheimer's and related dementias: the GREAT RCT. Health Technol Assess. 2019 Mar;23(10):1-242.)

Can someone on your team help you find a group such as the goal-oriented cognitive rehabilitation described in this work? Could they do the search for similar programs in your area or for occupational rehabilitation or social services programs? Does the local Alzheimer's Association or Area Agency on Aging have any information on something like this? Specifically, the program included "… the goals addressed in therapy related to engaging in activities, managing everyday tasks and situations, using appliances and devices, being well-oriented, retaining or keeping track of information and events, locating belongings, recognizing, identifying and naming people and objects, engaging in conversation, keeping in contact with family and friends, being organized, managing emotions, and basic self-care." The study's authors found that the intervention helped with the process of psychological adjustment to living with dementia, leading to feelings of greater confidence, less anxiety and better coping skills.

Can people on your team begin to assist you in looking for programming that would interest you? Start with senior centers – do they offer outings and activities that you may enjoy? Do they have classes that might springboard into a new passion or interest? Activities that tap into your creativity or opinions are likely best, not activities that focus most on your memory. Is there transportation to the activity? Can you begin to explore using public transportation? Can you explore using a service such as Uber or taxi? Set some of this learning up early so that you can continue for longer into cognitive loss.

Is there a program that connects culture and seniors? A program called Connet2Culture,[179] facilitated by CaringKind in New

---

179 https://www.caringkindnyc.org/socialengagement/

York City, has many activities each month that are facilitated by the cultural institution and geared to those with cognitive loss so that the meetings are off-hours when things are quieter, with the focus on opinion and less on memory. Look for a similar program in your area.

Also, can people on your team begin to help you find assistance to help with other aspects of life that begin to unravel? Can you help by beginning to find or coordinate a handyperson doing multi-step maintenance tasks? Many programs that assist individuals to stay in their own home have a handyperson to fix/attend to and maintain situations that either become unsafe to perform or are unsafe if not attended to. At times, these services can be subsidized for seniors by local grants, and in some areas, there are vetted services available through a not-for-profit called Umbrella (available in the Capital region of New York state – more information at www.theumbrella.org). There is a fee for joining but may be something worthwhile for you or you are able to recreate. Can you find something similar in your area?

Transportation

"For a while Anytown, USA, keeps rolling by. But finally – a boxy two-story building differentiates itself from its look-alike neighbors: the dentist where Newton had his wisdom teeth out. Trip-trap, trip-trap. Just half a block to the Sizzler. Up goes the troll. He goes SPLASH in the water. Right angle, 10 blocks to the light on 300 East. Big nanny goat Gruff is over the bridge."[180]

We often overlook the complexity of transportation, but it actually involves many different skills. First, we need to

---
180 Saunders, Gerda. Memory's Last Breath (pp. 176-177). Hachette Books. Kindle Edition.

remember where we are going. Then, we must be able to read a map and navigate through a constantly changing environment. Finally, we must have quick reflexes to control the vehicle and respond to unexpected situations. For this reason, to state the obvious, driving can be dangerous and is therefore considered a privilege rather than a right.

Deciding when to stop driving is one of the most difficult discussions for individuals with dementia, as driving must stop for almost everyone with this illness. It is recommended to assess the person's driving safety and plan for the loss of driving privileges as early as possible in the course of the disease. Regular reassessment should also be conducted.

"Predicting who can drive well and who cannot by assessing cognition in the physician's office is difficult, but factors that can help determine whether driving is potentially unsafe include the following: A low score on office-based memory testing or indicators of increasing difficulty with accomplishing normal day-to-day activities Perception of the driver's safety by a reliable caregiver who often accompanies the patient as a passenger. If a family member or care partner has avoided being a passenger in a car driven by the patient, was it because of concern for safety? Review your driving record, including minor accidents, tickets, and unexplained dents and scratches. Small dings on a bumper are common and may not be the driver's fault but scrapes or larger dents are more concerning. Multiple accidents and severe cognitive impairment. These are the clearest indicators for a physician to determine that driving is unsafe." [181]

---

[181] Noble, James M.. Navigating Life with Dementia (Brain and Life Books) (p. 187). Oxford University Press. Kindle Edition

Losing the ability to drive can mean a host of changes to the person living with dementia. Many individuals know when to give up driving due to safety. Several of the voices you've heard throughout this book have done just that: Richard Taylor, Wendy Mitchell, Greg O'Brien, Peter Berry. If you are uncertain, have a driving assessment done and repeat the driving test often. The driving assessment consists of two tests: one covering knowledge of road rules, which includes a short memory assessment, and a second one that involves driving or a simulated virtual evaluation.

After a formal driving assessment is completed, one of several formal determinations is made:

- Safe to continue driving; no remediation is necessary.
- Safe to continue driving, but some remediation is recommended to address minor problems.
- Unsafe to drive but skills may improve with training; a driving skills course can be tried, but driving is not allowed until proven successful.
- Unsafe to drive and skills will not improve; no remediation plan is recommended.

My mother was reluctant to discontinue driving but did not want to harm another if she was deemed unsafe. She had her driving evaluated on an annual basis. The first time that a test came back requesting that she perform some remediation, she was devastated. She understood that her skills were slipping but could not fathom what would happen if she could not drive independently. It was at this time when she considered a move to assisted living in a more positive light, so that she would have access to their transportation and socialization resources.

It is important to be safe, but far more important to begin planning what will substitute for the driving – whether it is relying on friends and family, hiring a driver, training to use something like taxis or a driving service such as Uber, learning a public transportation system if one is available, or moving to a housing situation that supports your transportation needs.

Medication/Medical Coordination

"From then on, you live every day in the glare of a crossing-over that will happen in a designated time frame. If your diagnosis stems from a physically morbid disease, your focus will likely be on how best to control your pain and other aspects of your journey to death. If your fate is dementia, you focus on the fact by the time the disease has taken you to a 'natural' death, your mind will have died long ago. You will have become 'simultaneously life and death incarnate.' After my dementia diagnosis, I took Hirst's shark very personally: not only something, but also someone could be there and not there at the same time. And that someone: me."[182]

In this section, I am going to focus on discussion to support your end-of-life choices. There is more to be said about handling your medications and modifying or limiting your healthcare choices, but I feel this has been covered in other areas of the book, and if you can have discussions about end-of-life choices, you can have less emotionally charged discussion about handling medications or healthcare choices.

---

182 Saunders, Gerda. Memory's Last Breath (p. 222). Hachette Books. Kindle Edition

Supporting Your End-of-Life Choices

Whether you agree or disagree with your family members about issues of your health and safety, the conversation needs to occur so that you can deepen your relationship and make your wishes known. Your family members may not want to have the conversation with you. Many people are uncomfortable discussing sensitive topics. Look for signs that the time might not be right, such as hesitation, guarded answers, attempts to change the subject, or possibly converting to charged or absolutes in the conversations such as "I hate speaking about this," "I never want to discuss this with you," or "You *always* get so morbid." Don't be put off by their discomfort but use the reluctance to show compassion and gently and firmly ask for contemplation and a follow-up time to discuss. You may soften the approach by beginning with, "I know this is going to be a challenging conversation and it is important to me. If this is not a good time, let's schedule a time in the near future." Do your best to keep the conversation as neutral as possible. Try not to tread into their emotional trigger points if you know what they are.

It's helpful to start with understanding. For example, you may begin with, "I know you're not interested in talking about death and ..." or "I understand that you may find this disease distressing but ..." You can then make your points from there. It's helpful to put boundaries around the problem. Try to look for places where you agree. For example, you could begin with "We both love each other very much. And the thought of losing one another is heartbreaking."

And then pause and listen for their response. Sometimes it's good to remember to talk less and allow for some breaks in

ENGAGING WITH FAMILY AND THE HEALTHCARE SYSTEM

the conversation so that your conversation partner can process and formulate a response. Experts believe that you should try to take the word "but" out of many of these conversations as that is a negative or subtracting sign in a conversation, often "erasing" what was just said.

You can try "... and at the same time" or begin a question with "What do you think?" Remember that when you hear "Yes, but" it may seem that somebody is trying to win the conversation rather than have a conversation.

Finally, if possible, tell a story. To help elucidate your points, bring it back to times when you've agreed on things.

You may want to practice some of these stories, and remember, you can always put a placeholder in and say, "We've talked about a lot today. I would really love to think about this more and come back to this conversation. Would that be okay with you?"

I love the information that Gerda Saunders put together to guide her family. I think that the list is approachable, can guide people, and addresses her specific concerns but without being too scary. Consider using her list and modifying it to your needs.

- Do I wake up most days feeling joyful and excited about my new day, no matter the level of intellectual activity I am capable of?
- Do I look forward to more things than I dread?
- Do I appear and act happy for more hours per day than I appear and act unhappy?
- Do I complain frequently about loneliness, depression, or boredom?
- Do I sleep most of the day?

- Am I insatiable in my needs and demands of my caretakers, be they family or care-center personnel?
- Does it take my combined caretakers more hours per day to care for me than the hours when I am not consuming care?
- Should I be at home, is/are my primary caretaker(s) stressed and worn out and constantly on the edge of a breakdown?
- Do I enjoy being in my garden (or that of the care center) watching the plants, birds, insects? Can I physically get there without needing a team of people?
- Are my caretakers' children or jobs or quality of life suffering as a result of their care for me?
- Do my family members feel I am still within the boundaries of a meaningful life as they have seen me living it over the years? Do I give comfort to my friends, children, and grandchildren, or am I disturbed by their presence and suspicious of their intentions?
- Do I revert to the racism I learned as a child in apartheid South Africa (as my mother did)?
- Am I physically approachable without getting myself into a state of fear or anger; that is, is it still a pleasure for me to cuddle with a friend or child or grandchild? In other words, do I still provide (and enjoy) "the comfort of a warm body?"[183]

---

[183] Saunders, Gerda. Memory's Last Breath (p. 249-250). Hachette Books. Kindle Edition.

Administration/Finances

How do you bring someone in to safeguard your financial situation? Much like speaking of death, this is an area where many of us don't discuss this topic with others, don't really want others "in our business," and don't really want to be told how to use our finances. Much like driving, finances are a key to our independence.

That being said, it is also an area where cognitive loss can render us vulnerable to poor judgements, not due to our ability to make "good" judgment, but by the loss of brain cells that may connect the process of making logical judgements.

People who have dementia may be vulnerable to financial exploitation or mismanagement of money in situations such as being unable to visit the bank without help, having many caregivers, being repeatedly contacted by scammers, or leaving money and financial documents out in the open at home.

How can you accept help in this area? Examples include having a responsible, trusted family member (or other) to help you manage your finances, scheduling payment of bills, sharing access to online banking information, and having a co-signer on joint accounts. Setting up a safe system with an experienced elder-care lawyer or tax attorney may assist you in minimizing financial risk. There are several strategies that may be worthwhile to protect you from scams and fraud, such as implementing a credit card fraud notification to you and a trusted family member if charges exceed a capped amount or for suspicious activity. There are a multitude of horror stories of individuals losing their hard-earned nest-egg to unscrupulous predators.

Connecting with Healthcare

What is the goal for speaking with your healthcare team? In an article by a team of researchers from the University of California San Francisco, persons living with dementia were asking for a therapeutic alliance. A therapeutic alliance is formed between a medical provider and a patient when they both agree on treatment goals and the necessary tasks to achieve those goals, while also having a personal connection. "Alliances between healthcare providers and patients can have a positive impact on health outcomes by improving adherence to care plans, reducing anxiety, and promoting better self-care. The provider's ability to demonstrate empathy is essential in creating these alliances. Skilled use of empathy during difficult conversations can reduce patient anxiety and increase adherence to treatment plans and self-care by building trust. … Failing to initiate conversations about diagnosis, support, and future outcomes may contribute to patients' unaddressed fears and feelings of distress."[184]

Be direct – let your healthcare provider know that you want and need information, and that you want your family or another to be involved, so that these discussions and understandings can continue if or as your cognitive loss progresses.

Is Healthcare Even the Right Place to Address Care?

Many would say to focus more on the social aspects, as the medical issues are limited in focus and scope. I would not

---

[184] Portacolone E, Covinsky KE, Johnson JK, Halpern J. Expectations and Concerns of Older Adults With Cognitive Impairment About Their Relationship With Medical Providers: A Call for Therapeutic Alliances. Qual Health Res. 2020 Aug;30(10):1584-1595. doi: 10.1177/1049732320925796. Epub 2020 Jun 20. PMID: 32564681; PMCID: PMC7398607

disagree with this. At the same time, it is important to have a multi-pronged approach to managing cognitive loss, including the allegiance and support of your healthcare providers.

Regarding healthcare, find someone that knows dementia. If there is no one in your area, use an up-to-date trusted book such as Navigating Life with Dementia by James Noble, MD, or follow a reputable site, such as mine.[185]

The benefits of a book such as Navigating Life with Dementia is that it provides an overview of what is needed in one place. Especially helpful in Navigating Life with Dementia is chapter 12 on "Lifestyle Management and Nonpharmacological Therapies for People with Dementia and their Caregivers". Dr. Noble recommends developing a plan of care, as we have in this book, regarding addressing values/strategies to support moving into later stages, adjusting your diet to be heart-healthy, minimizing alcohol intake in the face of a diagnosis of dementia, exercising in moderation, and remaining socially and cognitively engaged.

"Healthcare providers may assist in finding professional care providers. The referral may highlight the following concerns:

- Home safety, such as risk of falls, cooking safety, and medication supervision, particularly during times when the patient is alone.
- Skilled nursing needs, such as delivery of injections (e.g., insulin for diabetics), wound care, or instruction in how to use medical assistive devices.

---
[185] https://togetherindementia.com

- Unskilled needs, such as care coordination to ensure appointments are kept, shopping, cooking, housecleaning, or coordination of other daily tasks."[186]

Choosing a Healthcare Provider to Speak With

Many physicians are never trained in geriatric medicine, its philosophy or its tenets. And not all geriatric physicians are trained in palliative care. They are very good physicians, but their focus is not in this area. What I put forth here will be from my perspective as both a geriatrician and palliative care physician. If you agree with my perspective, you may have to advocate for this approach with the healthcare system.

Why do I say this as a geriatrician and palliative care physician? I have had encounters when nurses, advanced practice nurses, physician's assistants, and other physicians disagree with a palliative approach as an individual transitions from moderate- to late-stage dementia. I should say that I don't get similar pushback from the social workers or chaplains in hospitals, long-term care, or community.

Many healthcare workers do not realize that dementia is both a chronic and a terminal disease, and they are often not aware of the signs and symptoms of late-stage dementia. They do not realize that limiting medical interventions while providing excellent care is associated with higher ratings of quality of life for patients and caregivers and less stress, anxiety, and depression for caregivers. And if they asked what most people wanted, they would find that most people would choose a more measured approach, as Gerda Saunders describes. "However,

---

[186] Noble, James M. Navigating Life with Dementia (Brain and Life Books) (p. 176). Oxford University Press. Kindle Edition.

my preliminary research confirmed what Peter and I had learned anecdotally: no existing medications could stave off the inevitable decline that catches up with even the most diligently monitored patient. We were afraid that the quest for diagnosis could trap us in what writer and physician Atul Gawande once described as 'the unstoppable momentum of medical treatment.' Still, we are both the kind of people who want to know, always drawn like moths toward enlightenment. Also, confirmation of our suspicions might help us prepare. If the unnamable loomed ahead, we could plan for expensive care, diminished quality of life, and a way to end my life at the right time."[187]

How do you know if your physician agrees with you? Ask them for their usual approach to care of their patients with dementia. Do they refer individuals with dementia for hospice? If so, what triggers these referrals? Would they be willing to support you in your end-of-life wishes as you develop them? Will they work with your chosen surrogate decision-maker? Your questions may assist them in broadening their own perspective.

Compassion and Choices has an excellent physician communication worksheet.[188] They recommend making a special, stand-alone visit with your primary care physician (which is covered by Medicare to be billed via planning for advance directives). They recommend asking these following questions:

1. "When making treatment recommendations, will you be honest about their impact on my quality of life? And will you honor my decision if I choose quality-of-life over quantity?"

---

187 Saunders, Gerda. Memory's Last Breath (pp. 7-8). Hachette Books. Kindle Edition
188 https://compassionandchoices.org

2. "I have filled out a dementia addendum to my advance directive. It specifies the point at which I would wish to forgo human interventions that could extend my life (e.g., breathing support, cardiac pacing, antibiotics, or force feeding). Should this time ever come, are you willing to support me and my designated advocate?"

3. "Do you follow any religious or ethical directives when making treatment recommendations? If so, how would that impact my care? And are you associated with any health system or hospital that requires you to abide by such directives?"

4. "If the option of medical aid in dying is legally available in this state and I meet the eligibility criteria, will you honor my request for a prescription under this law?"

If they cannot support you, can your neurologist or a geriatrician? If you cannot find a physician to support your wishes, I recommend you state your end-of-life wishes very clearly in a document or video and add your wishes as a codicil to your living will. Many of the problems near the end of life can be avoided by avoiding hospitalizations, tube feeding, CPR and intubation. Be very clear on your stance on any or all of these interventions.

If your physician is willing to work with you, think through what you might want for an ideal, therapeutic alliance. What does that look like for you? Compassion and Choices has further resources available to help you in this partnership, something called a Trust Card™.[189] It asks you to select from a few choices described below, fill in your own thoughts, and care, to

---

189 https://usetrustcard.com/

be presented to your physician. The card can be generated for free or purchased for a small fee.

The topics that Compassion and Care Trust Card™[190] recommend contemplating are what would help you connect as people so your doctor can fully engage with you; a request to allow more time for questions; a request that the physician ask for your priorities and not make assumptions about them; request and encourage that everything is shared, not just the good news or the tests that she believes I need to know; request that the relationship is more of a partnership where decisions are made together; assure the physician that if you disagree, it isn't that you don't value their expertise or advice, just that you differ.

As Wendy Mitchell points out, you can adapt to a new way of thinking or a new physician or a new way of communicating with your physician because of the changes dementia brings – and that adaptation can be an improvement! "I've found myself reading and re-reading the same few pages, the plot never quite sticking in my head until I've given up altogether. It was hard giving up reading. I used to love getting lost in a good book. And yet, I knew there must be an alternative, that I didn't have to let it go altogether. Does it have to be so black and white, or could there be a middle ground? And then it came to me: I would switch from novels to short stories. I've never read many before, but they are more manageable, the characters who live for just a few pages sticking more firmly in my head, the anxiety of trying to remember their backstory gone from my

---

[190] https://usetrustcard.com/

chest. Reading is a pleasure again, now that I've thought of a way to adapt."[191]

Understanding Hospice

"Not that I plan a speedy exit, but just to have all the necessary discussions with Peter and the children and draw up a guide for Peter and the kids when the right time comes. In the end it will be their decision whether to assist me in my suicide (only in ways that are legal) or warehouse my emptied-out-head-attached-to-my-life-clinging-body until my strong heart stops."[192]

Hospice care is both a philosophy and a health care benefit. It focuses on the palliation of a person's pain and symptoms and attends to their emotional and spiritual needs at the end of life. Hospice care prioritizes comfort and quality of life by reducing physical, emotional, and spiritual pain and suffering. Hospice care avoids life-prolonging measures that may cause more symptoms or are not aligned with a person's goals. It is often described as an extra layer of support for the person and family when a terminal illness reaches its final stages.

In the U.S., hospice is also a medical benefit covered by Medicare. Individuals require documentation by two physicians that the individual has approximately six months to live. This estimation is more difficult with dementia, so guidelines for inclusion in hospice are recommended for physicians to follow. The criteria are outlined in Table 3 to help guide you in communicating with your family and your physician. Many primary care physicians are unaware of the criteria, as hospice is often underutilized.

---

[191] Mitchell, Wendy. Somebody I Used to Know (p. 95). Random House Publishing Group. Kindle Edition.
[192] Saunders, Gerda. Memory's Last Breath (p. 237). Hachette Books. Kindle Edition.

Hospice benefits include access to a multidisciplinary treatment team who specialize in end-of-life care and can be accessed in the home, long-term-care facility, or the hospital, though individuals with dementia rarely need or qualify for inpatient hospital admission. Hospice can provide durable medical supplies such as hospital beds and wheelchairs as well as supplement with home health aides, volunteers, and companions.

Individuals with dementia often do not activate their hospice benefit. The reasons are likely varied, but this area has not been well researched. In my conversations with both families and physicians, they report not understanding that dementia would be an eligible diagnosis, thinking that hospice mostly serves those with cancer.

Studies show that primary care physicians and physician extenders (e.g., nurse practitioners, physician assistants) don't often know when cognitive loss becomes eligible for hospice. Improving education to these groups has been helpful in increasing the participation, but the education and interest may not reach your area in time to help you.

For this reason, it may be important for you or your family to know when to ask for a referral. Studies also show that individuals and families are ready to discuss advance care planning but are often waiting for the healthcare provider to bring it up. Those individuals and families who take the time and have the courage to discuss their advance care planning feel relief and less anxiety, knowing that their opinions and wishes have been stated and recorded.

Hospice care provides a layer of support in the form of nursing staff in the home or at the end of the phone line to answer medical questions that arise often. The nursing component can supplement aides to assist with personal care and respite. There is social worker support, for legal, systems, and benefit questions, but also for counseling and emotional support. There are spiritual personnel for issues of faith, existential questions. and prayers. Finally, volunteers can add layers of richness with reading, art, pet therapy, or companionship.

Prognostication is not perfect in dementia care, so that the risk of "graduating" from hospice is present and may occur when patients plateau or show little decline. One article in the medical literature calls it getting "expelled," and they are correct.[193]

Hopefully, by the time hospice care is needed, the system will have addressed the need for prolonged exposure as the layer of support is likely a large part of the reason for the plateau. I recently had to "graduate" or "expel" a 107-year-old woman from our hospice program. She had significant pain, had side effects from too many medications, and was feeling depressed when my team met her. We were able to address her pain, remove side effects by limiting her medications to only those that addressed her pain, and began counseling and pain management for her depression so that her mood lifted considerably, and her appetite returned. These interventions stopped her physical/emotional decline and her health stabilized. We were all sorry to stop our work with her, and she said, "I will miss you girls!" Her family will do their best to keep her socialization up and are happy to know what helped so that they can implement similar strategies, but they are also discouraged to

---

[193] Hunt LJ, Harrison KL. Live discharge from hospice for people living with dementia isn't "graduating"-It's getting expelled. J Am Geriatr Soc. 2021 Jun;69(6):1457-1460. doi: 10.1111/jgs.17107. Epub 2021 Apr 14. PMID: 33855701; PMCID: PMC8192462.

lose our expertise to improve the quality of life for their mother. Regardless, they said they were happy they called hospice in, even if they lost these services down the road. We will be happy to go back in anytime they need us again!

What are the myths about hospice that must be overcome so that you or your family don't miss this amazing benefit?

Hospice is giving up: Nothing could be further from the truth! Hospice is doing more. It is shifting the focus of care, but not stopping care. It may be stopping some futile medical interventions, but it is increasing the care that improves quality of life. The goal would be to widen one's view to ask more questions about the goals the person would like to accomplish, and what would increase peace, comfort, and understanding. I find that it is more leaning in than giving up!

Hospice is only for cancer patients: When hospice began in the U.S. in the 1970s, it did focus on cancer patients. Hospice now has criteria for several medical conditions, and only about 30 percent of hospice admissions are for cancer.[194] Unfortunately, admissions for dementia continue to remain low, but hopefully by reading this and contemplating your own options, you will see the benefit of adding hospice to your planning.

Hospice is where you go to die: I admit I am often surprised when I hear this, but it is a commonly held belief. In fact, most people receive care wherever they live, which includes private residences, assisted living communities, hospitals, and long-term-care facilities. In very rare cases, when pain cannot be well controlled at home, someone may be transferred to an inpatient hospice – these people usually have some type of cancer pain.

---

194 https://www.nhpco.org/hospice-facts-figures/

Hospice means I'm going to die soon: This is definitely not true. Studies show that although hospice care neither hastens death nor prolongs life, people live somewhat longer with hospice care than those with the same illness who don't choose hospice care. Most importantly, satisfaction with services received are consistently higher when hospice is involved.

You can't keep your own doctor if you enter a hospice program: Your physician is encouraged to remain engaged in your care. The hospice physician should work with your physician to coordinate your care.

It is the doctor's responsibility to bring up hospice: While it is the physician's responsibility to determine whether a patient meets the medical eligibility criteria to receive hospice services, it is appropriate for the patient (or caregiver) to initiate the discussion. Many patients and families report they wish they had received hospice sooner. It is OK to tell your physician or any other healthcare personnel that you are open to discussing hospice care, even as early as when you receive your diagnosis, so that you've opened the door for when the time is right. If you think the time is right to begin hospice, but your physician isn't sure, please ask for a hospice evaluation. The hospice team can guide you and then guide the physician regarding the specific criteria.

Once you choose hospice care there is no turning back: You are free to leave a hospice program at any time for any reason without penalty, and you can re-enroll in a hospice program any time that you meet the medical eligibility criteria. I've had people revoke their hospice benefit for a brief period to obtain a procedure or therapy that wouldn't be covered, and quickly resume the hospice program once that procedure was completed.

If you choose hospice care, you won't get other medical care: The hospice team will provide all aspects of care for the qualifying illness and will discuss what aspects of that care you do or don't want to receive. If you choose to have other medical care, you have all rights to seek that care and be covered by your non-hospice Medicare insurance. The team will be available to discuss with you whether that care aligns with your overall wishes. The most common example that comes up is, "What if I break my hip from a fall – can I still go to the hospital to have that taken care of so that I'm not in pain?" Absolutely! That is a perfect example of receiving care that may fall outside of the hospice benefit.

Hospice requires a DNR (Do Not Resuscitate) Order: The purpose and benefit of hospice care is to allow for a peaceful passing in a comfortable and familiar setting like home with loved ones near. While many people wish to have a DNR to avoid unnecessary medical intervention and hospitalization, you are not required to have a DNR to receive hospice care.

All hospices are the same: There are many hospices and each have their own personality. They may be not-for-profit or for-profit; hospital-based or community-based; independent or linked to a larger organization – each will bring certain strengths and weaknesses. If they participate in Medicare, they are required to provide certain services and documentation. You may interview many, choose one, and if not happy, switch to another. Find what is right for you.

What If My Doctor Says It Is Not Time?

Healthcare staff have a difficult time predicting upcoming death in those living with late-stage dementia. They expected only one percent of these nursing home residents with dementia to die in the next six months, but 71 percent of those individuals died during this period.[195]

You may therefore need to ask specifically for a hospice referral. Educate yourself and your family about this. In the table below are the criteria for hospice admission.

I can tell you that when I requested that hospice be started for my mother, I received pushback from her primary care physician (and my friend and colleague) and the home health aides at her assisted-living residence. All felt I was "giving up" too early. I informed them all that I was not giving up at all but living within our values. The values were to focus on comfort and home, not on interventions that had limited or, worse, adverse effects. It was through watching my mother have brief, calm ups and downs in her final years that the physician and aides came to thank me for requesting hospice. The assisted-living residence began to ask for hospice more often once they saw the decrease in frequent trips to the emergency room for difficulty swallowing, pneumonia, fevers, or falls.

As this entire book has been saying, decide on your choices and then educate yourself and your healthcare provider on how to make these values be a living example in your life.

---

[195] Mitchell SL, Kiely DK, Hamel MB. Dying with advanced dementia in the nursing home. Arch Internal Med (2004) 164(3):321–6

Table 3: Hospice Criteria for Admission for Dementia

1. Stage 7 on FAST Scale – A, B, and C criteria are critical indicators of end-stage Alzheimer's disease. Additional criteria lend additional support to terminal status:	• Incontinence • Inability to communicate meaningfully (one to five words a day) • Non-ambulatory (unable to ambulate and bear weight) • All intelligible vocabulary lost • Unable to sit up independently • Unable to smile • Unable to hold head up
2. Presence of co-morbid disease distinct from the terminal illness will impact functional impairment. The combined effects of Alzheimer's and any co-morbid condition should support a prognosis of six months or less.	• Chronic obstructive pulmonary disease (COPD) • Congestive heart failure (CHF) • Cancer • Liver disease • Renal failure • Neurological disease

3. Patients should have had one of the following secondary conditions within the past 12 months:	• Delirium • Recurrent or intractable infections, such as pneumonia or other upper respiratory infection • Pyelonephritis or other urinary tract infection • Septicemia • Decubitus ulcers, multiple stages 3-4 • Fever, recurrent after antibiotics • Inability to maintain sufficient fluid and calorie intake demonstrated by either of the following: 10 percent weight loss during the previous six months or serum albumin <2.5 gm/dl • Aspiration pneumonia

Ideas for How to Have a Hospice Conversation with Your Team, Your Family, Your Health Care Proxy, and/or Your Physician

Have a dinner with family or your healthcare proxy. Ask questions of their perception of hospice. Do they have concerns? Do they have questions about what happens? I find that when these concerns and questions can be addressed, most people see the philosophical advantages to hospice. The next issue to address is their reluctance to allow someone to die. That usually takes some reflection on their part, and then the inevitability of life and death will sink in, and most will shift to feeling their grief, rather than resisting it. Stories that can help with grief and loss may assist as well, as most of us feel better when we are not alone. There can be several choices, but Leo Tolstoy's *The Death of Ivan Ilych"* and Stephen Crane's *The Open Boat* are two short stories that are often cited to assist in placing death in the grander frame of life.

For healthcare providers, Compassion and Choices[196] offers a letter that may be used as a template in crafting a letter to your own primary care physician. It is found on page 33 of the online document.

Points to Remember

- To maintain your independence as long as possible, you will need to begin to communicate your needs and wants to other who can assist you on your journey.
- Family/friends may become too "paternalistic" due to their preconceived notions about cognitive loss.
- Layers of support will need to be added as cognitive loss advances.
- Building a team for adding layers of support should begin now.
- Areas that will likely need support are socializing and adapting to cognitive loss; transportation; medical and medication coordination, specifically supporting your end-of-life choices; finances and administrative tasks.
- Realize that most of the decisions needed for your life with dementia will not be focused on medicine and look for support outside the medical field – the psychological and social

---

[196] https://compassionandchoices.org

and humanistic aspects have been covered throughout this book.
- The healthcare system is behind in the humanistic approach to care concerning dementia – know that you may be educating and guiding them.
- Palliative care is a philosophy and hospice is the medical benefit to be implemented in the last several months of life to make quality and comfort priorities.

Action Plan

- Begin to make a list of how you imagine others can help you now and as your function begins to decline.
- Consider who can assist you in a facilitated talk to begin to train your family or at least your primary care partner regarding the balance between autonomy and support without the partner taking too much control. Teach them the MacArthur Competence Assessment Tool so that they can separate when to support and not take over.
- Use the guidelines in the chapter to begin to build a team of support – then address plans for socialization; transportation; medical coordination; finances and administration needs that are current and likely the next issues forthcoming.
- Do you have a therapeutic alliance with your healthcare team? If not, begin to build one or find a team you are comfortable building this trust with. Utilize the toolkit from Compassion and Choices to assist you.

- Make sure that you have made clear to your family when you would like to switch to medical care focused on comfort rather than cure and have them advocate for beginning hospice as soon as is possible.

Resources

Gerda Saunders, Memory's Last Breath.

This memoir, of Ms. Saunders' life, her passion for literature, science, parenting and travel, her deep love and commitment in her marriage is melded into thoughtful, honest and raw interpretation of her changing self. She reveals joy, life, perseverance, thoughtfulness, reflection, communication and controversy. It is an interesting read and the ending - that focuses on her choices for end-of-life contemplation and decisions are honest and direct.

James M Noble, MD, MS, CPH, FAAN, Navigating Life with Dementia (Brain and Life Books)

This is a helpful guide for individuals with dementia, as well as their friends and families. It provides tools to manage daily challenges and prepare for the long-term impact of the disease. The book covers various stages of the disease, from early signs of cognitive problems to advanced stages, and offers easy-to-understand explanations of the complexities of dementia. It also discusses how to establish a diagnosis and provides advice on how to anticipate and manage common problems.

Made in the USA
Middletown, DE
30 July 2024